THE CHEEKY GUIDE TO OXFORD

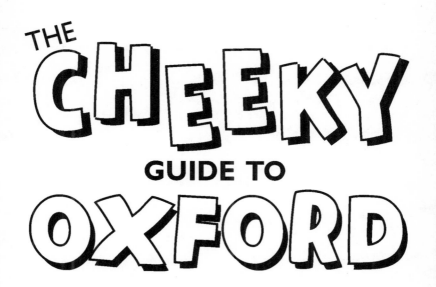

THE CHEEKY GUIDE TO OXFORD

GUIDE TO

Written by David Bramwell

Researched by David Bramwell,
Richard Hadfield and Jeremy Plotnikoff

Illustrations by Lisa Holdcroft

Collages by Al Cane

The Cheeky Guide To Oxford
Written by David Bramwell
Researched by David Bramwell, Jeremy Plotnikoff and Richard Hadfield

ISBN 0 9536110 1 9
Published in 2000 by
cheekyguides Ltd
72 Buckingham Rd
Brighton BN1 3RJ
Business enquiries: jeremy@cheekyguides.com
Comments or suggestions: david@cheekyguides.com

Acknowledgements
Thanks to Justin Time, Bill Heine, Mog, Paul from Undercurrents, Robin Darwall-Smith, Mrs Butler, Sarah Bendall, Anu, Chris, Harriet, Anna, Debs for late night sanity restoration, everyone at Nightshift, Elizabeth Boardman, Billie Pink, Carina aka Hamster, Paul & Charlotte, Alex Ogg, Serina, Siobhan and Charlie and anyone else we met along the way who gave us a good story or two. I apologise in advance for any deviation of the truth in anything you might have told me. It is a Cheeky Guide after all.

Special thanks to Jane, Pete, Steve and Ellie for their B&B skills, support and forever persuading us that going for a drink was much more agreeable than staying in and writing. Apologies to Jane for wetting your bed that night.

Artwork
A big thank-you to Lisa Holdcroft for the cover, the map, the innumerable cartoons and taking it all in her stride when we'd phone her up at two in the morning demanding a cartoon of a box with a unicorn's penis in it. For more information or just to tell her how talented she is contact (01273) 705658.
Al Cane provided the wonderfully bizarre collages that surely come from a disturbed mind. Look out for his colour postcards in different shops around town. For more info on Al contact visual99@hotmail.com
Acknowledgement to Allen Miles the co-author of the Cowley Road Beach picture.

Editing
Alex and Stephie did a heroic job editing this book. Thanks to Alex for offering good advice (like 'that's not funny get rid of it') and feeding me when really it was my turn to cook.

About the Creators of this Book

David Bramwell

Raised by his adopted parents on a strict diet of herring, David developed into a child prodigy and had already, by the age of four, realised that external forces were at play in the Sooty Show.

He graduated from Christ Church at only nine years old and went on to become one of the top Mathematics lecturers at the University, despite not having followed the more traditional route of developing a drink and hygiene problem first.

Disillusionment with vector diagrams and complex matrices soon set in however and he quit his job, spending the next few years drifting in and out of employment until he finally hit rock bottom playing the part of a Cyberman, alongside Bonny Langford in a Doctor Who musical.

The idea for Cheeky Guides came along at a crucial moment, as hard times, despair and deteriorating health had brought him dangerously close to accepting a job at the gift shop in the Oxford Story.

Being the principle writer and researcher of the book, David is, of course, the one who gets all the blame if someone isn't happy with their review, and only recently one disgruntled restaurateur threatened to 'hunt him down like a pig' for derogatory comments about his Eggs Benedict.

David lives in Brighton because it's nicer than Oxford but visits at weekends and recently bought himself a holiday home in nearby Blackbird Leys.

Jeremy Plotnikoff

Part Scottish, part Canadian and built entirely of Lego, Jeremy is easy to spot in the streets of Oxford owing to his angular red plastic body and large yellow head. For years he baffled scientists with his ability to whistle two-part harmonies at the same time until it was later discovered that someone was hiding in his trousers.

A workaholic, Jeremy regularly toils round the clock, culminating in extensive sleep deprivation, and in the final throws of creating this book he entered states of consciousness previously only dreamed about by William Burroughs and became convinced that a herd of giant pandas were throwing Garibaldi biscuits at him, which largely accounts for all the spelling mistakes.

After the success of the first Cheeky Guide, Jeremy abandoned his wife and kids and shacked up with 80s sex-kitten Linda Lusardi. Although they now live together in a luxury penthouse apartment in Florida, he hasn't forgotten his roots and still pops back to Oxford now and again to pick up his royalties from the book.

Jeremy is responsible for the layout and design of this book as well as fiddling the accounts, lying to publishers and implementing crude torture techniques on any potential competitors. Despite all this he has a nice smile and is a vegetarian.

Richard Hadfield aka Dippy

Handsome, gifted and rich, Dippy is not known for any of these qualities but does, however, have a rare talent for opening beer bottles with his nostrils.

Despite the ridiculous nickname, his friends know him better as the Human Beat-Box. Give Dippy a microphone and he will provide hours of top-class entertainment with just some simple bass and snare sounds, although he has on occasions been known to throw in some fancy triplets on the hi-hat to woo the ladies.

Dippy joined the Cheeky team early last year after returning from South America where he had spent nine months in a Colombian prison as part of a work exchange programme.

A bit like Brains from Thunderbirds, Dippy is responsible for 'behind the scenes planning' in the Cheeky Empire and if we all become millionaires, we'll have him to thank. Having almost single-handedly reviewed the cafés and restaurants for the book as well, Dippy is an expert on where to get the best curry in Oxford but as a consequence is now a bit of a fatty.

He is happiest with a bottle of beer in one hand and a cricket bat in the other but often gets confused between the two, leading to disastrous consequences. He has lived in Oxford now for the last ten years with his ménagerie of Guinea fowl and his fiancée Jane who is a bandy-legged Capricorn.

In researching this book we have:

- witnessed the lone musician at a music evening in a pub pick a fight with a punter claiming — 'you called William the Conqueror's mother a bitch' before he was swiftly ejected.

- met a girl called Gill, in a certain shop, who was on probation for being rude to the customers. Having informed gullible Americans that they would need to march up and down to see if they were fit enough to do the walking tours, she would then proceed to measure their strides with a tape and then gravely announce her verdict.

- encountered a 50-year-old woman in knee-high green wellies dancing like Bez from the Happy Monday's on her own in an empty pub.

- tried to bribe our way into being an extra in an Inspector Morse episode being filmed outside Thornton's bookshop but got told to 'bugger off'.

- became too scared to meet one Oxford eccentric when it became apparent that the author of this book would have had to match him drink for drink in a whiskey session that would have no doubt led to his death.

- got arrested for driving down Broad Street at four in the morning, partly because it was illegal but, more importantly, because the policeman who had been sat in his car for five hours just wanted someone to talk to. He kept us there for 45 minutes nattering amiably about nothing in particular and then fined us £30.

- ...and Dippy got engaged. He was proposed to at 10.30pm in the Eagle Tavern (opposite the Magic Café) and Meatloaf was playing on the jukebox. Naturally he said 'Yes'.

We have toiled day and night to be accurate with prices, times of opening etc, but we're only human (except Jeremy who's Canadian) so if you spot any changes or mistakes, drop us a line and we'll be grateful. Gushing adoration in the form of gifts and money will also be warmly received.

Nobody paid to be reviewed in this book and with the exception of some Granola and several home-made biscuits, we haven't had any freebies.

I know, I know, what a wasted opportunity.

The **Cheeky**

CONTENTS

guide to Oxford

A Brief History of Oxford

Our story begins with a pious young lady called Frideswide, whose tale rather romantically marks the beginning of the town around the 7th century and is steeped in mystical and spiritual metaphors, as well as having been embellished for a good 1300 years.

Frideswide is said to have been a beautiful princess who, having reached that certain age, had an eager suitor in the shape of a king. Desiring only to embrace the spiritual life of a nun, and not wanting to spend her days launching ships and eating gala lunches, Frideswide ran away, first to Binsey wood and then to Oxford. Her regal suitor, having already sent out the wedding invitations and booked the jester, followed hot on her trail, determined to take her by force. As he approached Oxford's city gate, however, he was struck blind. Realising that being pushy early on in a relationship always leads to trouble, the foolish young king got down on his knees and begged the girl's forgiveness, at which she restored his sight (with a spot of good old fashioned fairy tale magic) providing they could just be friends.

Frideswide went on to set up Oxford's first nunnery on the sight of Christ Church Cathedral while The King found a niche in the market for black music sung by a white man.

The spiritual tone of the legend was not ill-founded however, for by the 13th century the college buildings as we now know them were starting to spring up as places for monastic scholars and Oxford soon became established as a city of religious learning. Only through a slow transformation over the centuries did other subjects eventually come to be studied here and even nowadays Media Studies is still frowned upon by most of the colleges as being too 'satanic'.

By the 14th century, as the colleges grew, relationships between the local people and the students (better known then as the Town and Gown) had soured to the point where animosity between the two was rife. Although they seem to tolerate each other nowadays and even occasionally inter-breed, a terrible battle between the two actually took place on February 10th 1355 and is still remembered today as St Scholastica's Day.

The story begins in Swindlestock tavern, an ale house in the city centre, where an argument between a student and the landlord over the quality of a glass of wine led to the student throwing the wine in the landlord's face and giving him a deadleg. A fight soon erupted between the two and before long a full scale brawl was taking place in the pub and then out on the streets with students, townsfolk and the odd tourist all joining in. By the end of the day, an uneasy truce between Town and Gown was eventually made and the colleges thought that that was the end of it.

The next morning, however, many of the townsfolk were still feeling bloodthirsty and so roped in hundreds of other laymen from the surrounding villages to help with their revenge. Woefully outnumbered this time, the students who didn't flee the city were systematically massacred and by the end of a two-day battle, over 60 had been killed. The king, having caught wind of what was going on the previous day, had sent orders for the massacre to stop; yet this had fallen on deaf ears. By way of punishment to the townsfolk, he made them pay an annual fine to the students and gave the colleges certain privileges which included the setting up of their own police force and free handguns for the students. The handgun law was finally abandoned in the 1960s when an Oriel student confused by his new shiny toy accidentally shot the college gardener, but every year on St Scholastica's Day the townsfolk of Oxford must still by law visit one college and kiss the feet of the first student they see.

Three hundred years later, one of the strangest events in Oxford's history took place when in the 1640s its citizens woke up one morning to find that overnight their house prices had doubled and a series of trendy grog bars had sprung up on the High Street. Rather surprisingly, Oxford had suddenly become the capital of England.

The decision had been made by Charles I, who moved his court here for three years to do battle with Cromwell and his parliament during the Civil War. For a while the king and queen moved to Christ Church but, not used to living in such poky and cramped conditions, found themselves forever fighting over the sock drawer and eventually the queen moved into nearby Merton College. For three years the town found itself (willingly or otherwise) aiding Charles' efforts to keep his power in the country.

It didn't go quite to plan however, and after Charles' head and body parted company Oxford quickly returned to its former glory. Meanwhile, plans for a metro system were quietly dropped and everyone started saying hello to each other on the streets again.

For the next 300 years the University colleges found themselves slowly being encroached upon by the ever-growing city. By the Second World War Oxford was nearly as important for car manufacturing as it was for education, but it was still its beauty and academic reputation that saved it from Hitler's bombs as he had set his heart on the city as the headquarters for his occupation of England.

Since then, the dominance of the University has given way further still to other businesses including, of course, tourism. This industry has grown to such an alarming extent that in summer, when the streets get too over-crowded, the council arranges for fleets of open-topped buses to collect visitors, where they are taken to the old disused prison and made into jam.

Although the University has consistently produced some of the country's best-known politicians, writers and poets, in recent years the city itself has been put on the map for producing some world-famous guitar bands. And for the last 13 years every granny in England has been glued to the TV (not literally) to witness John Thaw running like the clappers round Oxford, usually in search of a kebab. The success of Inspector Morse has brought the city a new kind of fame, revealing the lesser known corners of the city and bringing a new breed of tourist, which finally led one drinking establishment to proudly erect a plaque stating - *'Morse has never been filmed here.'*

How to get Here

BY CAR

You can get to Oxford from London or from the Midlands via the M40 motorway. Get off at Junctions 8 or 9, both of these run into the city centre. Once you're off the M25 the drive is about 30-40 minutes depending on how dilapidated your car is.

BY TRAIN

Most rail passengers tend to come via Paddington station in London; the trains are frequent but the times change seasonally, therefore it is always best to call first (0345 484950). Direct trains are available from cities other than London but more usually you'll end up routed through everywhere in England, Scotland, and Ireland before arriving in Oxford.

Virgin Trains
Contact: 0121 6547400; tickets (0345) 222333
www.virgintrains.co.uk
For ensuring you'll always get the cheapest train tickets try
www.thetrainsline.co.uk

BY BUS

Buses for Oxford leave from just outside Victoria station and there are a few companies that offer this service, the main two being the Oxford Tube (01865 772250) and the Oxford Express (01865 785400). The buses leave every 12 minutes during daytime hours and prices start at £6 for a one way, £7.50 for next day return and £9.50 for an open return. The service operates 24 hours a day, but it is best to check times if you are leaving in the wee hours.
If for whatever reason these two are not convenient then you can also try National Express.
(0990) 808080 or on the Web at http://www.nationalexpress.co.uk

TAXI

Only big show-offs do this, but if you really feel that public transport is beneath you then a taxi from London to Oxford will cost about £75.

PLANE

Getting Around

From Gatwick there is a direct bus to Oxford which takes about two hours. The service runs round the clock from the north and south terminals, and costs £18 single, £19 for a return and £21 for an open return. Taxis from Gatwick to Oxford cost £90.

From Heathrow there is a direct bus service which takes about 70 minutes. The service runs round the clock from the Central Bus station at the airport and costs £11 single, £12 next day return and £14 for an open return.

If you are going from Oxford to the airport then remember to get off at the Heathrow bus station for terminals 1,2,3 and to stay on the bus until terminal 4 if that's your final destination. If you wish to take a taxi from Oxford to Heathrow it will cost you approximately £55.

BY RIVER

Having two rivers and a canal passing through it means that Oxford is still often reached by boat. Barges, steamboats and canoes regularly bring the more adventurous travellers to the city, although parking is becoming an increasing problem and canoe theft is rife. Last year a Cambridge student, blown off course in his punt, was found close to a nervous breakdown having spent two days asking bemused passers-by where to find King's College.

Contentious issues #1: Traffic

To say that Oxford has a small traffic problem would be like saying that Pavarotti is a bit portly. This has been a thorn in the side of town planners, councillors, road users and pretty much anyone else you can think of for as long as anyone can care to remember. Oxford just wasn't designed for the motor car. Of course the obvious solution would be to knock down a few of the colleges and build some more roads to ease congestion, but for some reason not everyone is in favour of this.

In fact, for many years there has been pressure on Christ Church to allow a road through its meadow, but thankfully they're a stubborn lot and haven't given in to such a ludicrous idea.

In recent years more of the town centre has been pedestrianised making it a bit safer but for some reason everyone seems more annoyed than ever. If you want to have a long tedious conversation with a local resident then mention the traffic problem and watch them rant and rave for a good half-hour. A final word of warning; for many bus drivers in Oxford their sole purpose in life seems to be to reduce the number of residents and tourists as quickly and efficiently as possible, so watch yourself when crossing the roads, especially down at Carfax.

PARKING

If you need to park in town it'll cost you a few quid just for a couple of hours in most places. You can take your chances down St Giles where you'll be in the heart of the town but it's pretty expensive, usually full and you can only stay for a few hours. Your best bet is to head for the main parking areas in the west near the station and around Oxpen's Road and Norfolk Street, which will still deposit you pretty much in the centre of town.

There's also :
A big one behind the Westgate Centre
A medium sized one behind Gloucester Green (via Beaumont Street)
A smallish one behind Tesco's on the Cowley Road
Pay and Display on St Giles and St Clement's

A loophole in Oxford's parking strategy

Of course I shouldn't really tell you this but I'm going to anyway. Just by Magdalen bridge is an old disused fountain with space next to it that neatly fits one car and is free. Regularly used by wily drivers, they'll probably be annoyed that I've told you but anyone daft enough to try and park in Oxford needs all the help they can get.

If you are a day visitor to Oxford you could instead use the Park and Ride service rather than coming into the City and fighting for Oxford's four parking spaces. You will see signs for the Park and Ride on the ring road at:

Pear Tree (north)
  Seven Days per week
Redbridge (south)
  Seven Days per week
Thornhill (east)
  Monday – Saturday only
Seacourt (west)
  Monday – Saturday only
  If you need any more info on the Park and Ride then call (01865) 785400

CAR HIRE

All the main hire companies are represented in Oxford, all are similar in price and their numbers are overleaf. If you have no joy with any of these, then look up the yellow pages, as there are loads of others.

Hiring a car to visit outside Oxford is a great idea, using it to see the city is of course suicidal.

Hertz (01865) 319972
Avis (0870) 60 60 100 24 hour central
booking line
Budget (01865) 724884
Europcar (01865) 246373
A1 Self Drive (01865) 436500 From
£20 per day

BUSES

The bus service in Oxford is excellent,
and so it should be for all the arsing
about that they have done with the
roads. Most journeys around town will
cost you 80p, but sometimes I have
only been charged 60p for the
identical journey. As I am scared of
bus drivers, I have yet to discover
what the criteria for this is.

Buses leave everywhere often and
take you most places although the
flaw in the system seems to be that
you can't get from East Oxford to
North Oxford without changing in the
city centre. The one exception is the
number 7A and number 2, which go
all the way from Headington to
Kidlington via the Banbury Road.

The Oxford Bus Company
(01865) 785 400
www.oxfordbus.co.uk Sells a little
booklet with all the routes etc for
20p.

Stagecoach
(01865) 727000
www.stagecoach-oxford.co.uk
Both located at the bus station in
Gloucester Green.

TAXIS

Taxis are everywhere, and flagging
them down never seems to be much
of a problem unless you're trying to
find one at 2.05 am and you've got
sick down the side of your jacket.

Ordering a taxi from home seems
to be an entirely different situation and
on many occasions when I've called
one they have been late or just not
bothered showing up at all. If you have
an important engagement call three
companies and pray that at least one
will turn up on time.

*There are taxi ranks at the station, St
George's Place (Gloucester Green), St
Giles, Broad Street and on the High Street.*

001 Cabs (01865) 24 00 00
ABC Taxi (01865) 770077
City Taxi (01865) 201 201

BICYCLES

At the last count, official figures show that there are now more bicycles here than there are people to ride them. This is the proper way to travel round Oxford and there are a plethora of bike lanes, and streets laden with bike racks, for your convenience.

Bike rentals are available all over town and most shops will quote you for daily, weekly, monthly or term (12 week) rentals. Deposits are required by all, usually ranging between £50-£100. Make sure that the rental includes lock and lights.

Cycle King
128 – 130 Cowley Road
(01865) 728262
£10 p/d , £15 p/w,
£30 p/m,
£45 p/t (ex vat)

Bike Zone
Market Street
(Central Oxford)
(01865) 728877
£10 p/d , £20 p/w,
£50 p/t (inc vat)

Cyclo Analysts
150 Cowley Road
(01865) 424444
1-3 days £10, £16 p/w,
£40 p/m, £50 p/t

Here There & Everywhere

THE CITY CENTRE

A labyrinth of shops, colleges, pubs, restaurants, museums and other tourist attractions, Oxford city centre is compacted into little more than a few dozen or so roads. Not surprisingly then, during the tourist season, Oxford becomes ridiculously busy with crowds of visitors and EF students filling the main thoroughfares in the town and converging around the burger bars to sing their national anthem 'We will rock you.' College students and locals, exasperated with it all, when asked for the 15th time by a tourist 'where is the university?' will end up pointing down the Cowley Road or sending them to Freuds.

But if you're new to Oxford, don't worry, all is not lost. The city has so

The Bridge of Sighs

many secrets, beautiful buildings and places of interest that, despite the crowds, it is a pleasure simply to walk around and take it all in. At the turn of every corner you could stumble across anything from a museum of shrunken heads to a meadow of cows. There are towers to climb, theatres to visit, galleries to see, colleges to walk around, parks and gardens and plenty of quiet areas like Merton Street and Hollywell Street where you can get a real taste of the old city.

And, besides, you'd be surprised how little the residents of Oxford really know about their hometown. Most locals don't know one college from the next, and if you stopped and asked any student on Broad Street to point out the Spoon Museum, chances are, half of them wouldn't know where it is.

With the exception of some of the tackier tourist experiences, there is, perhaps surprisingly, an almost guarded discretion to many of the places of interest here. The colleges only open their gates to the public when it pleases them, while many of the museums and other buildings do very little in the way of making their presence felt. Without a guide book or insider knowledge, many of Oxford's best features could go unnoticed by someone new to the city. But it is precisely this discretion that has saved Oxford from becoming swallowed up entirely by the tourist industry. Despite the visitors, life goes on, even if yet another American has just stopped to ask someone where the university campus is.

Carfax

Carfax tower stands at the top of the High Street and, for some, marks the beginning of the end, as beyond it is the all-familiar world of shopping centres, chain stores and crowds. The pedestrianised roads of Cornmarket and Queen Street, which meet at Carfax, are little more than a grotesque array of bland retail shops and really ought to be removed and dropped in Stevenage. Popular spot for kamikaze visitors who will blindly step out in front of the speeding buses to take photos of their friends outside the Edinburgh wool shop.

Broad Street

There is no other street in Oxford that manages to encompass as much of the town's character as Broad Street. This short stretch is home to Trinity and Balliol College, a good many bookshops, tourist shops, museums, a couple of pubs, the Sheldonian Theatre and the Bodleian library.

Walk down it on a typical day and you'll see students milling in and out of the colleges whilst just across the road the waxwork dummy of a college professor is luring unwitting visitors into the Oxford Story for a truly forgettable experience.

father and son enjoying the May day celebrations

Tourist shops, selling everything from Teddy bears to sweatshirts, sit between the grandeur of old and new bookshops. Further down the road the carved heads outside the Sheldonian theatre keep a watchful eye. Take a walk down Broad Street any time of day and chances are you'll end up in somebody's holiday snaps.

In the centre of Broad Street is a cross, where three Protestant martyrs were burned alive in the 1550s during the reformation, for defying the very Catholic Queen Mary.

There still seems to be some discrepancy about the actual location of the executions however. Despite its official location, marked in the centre of the street, budding historian Kieran from nearby Thornton's bookshop assured me that the actual spot was just below the 'please leave your bags at the desk' sign by the till. Although, when quizzed as to the exact date of the execution he told me with confidence that it was 'definitely pre-Beatles'.

If you need feeding and watering, the White Horse is a good spot for an afternoon's drink, caffeine addicts might like to know that upstairs in the big Blackwell's is an excellent coffee shop that does good sandwiches.

A few summers ago I remember a student used to appear on Broad Street every weekend and sit outside the Sheldonian Theatre specifically for the tourists to take pictures of him. He would always turn up wearing a three-piece tweed suit, clutching a walking stick and with a monocle stuffed in his

Australian students go in search of Cowley Beach

right eye. Then he'd sit down with his legs crossed, get out a copy of Ulysses and start to read.

I, like most onlookers, presumed he was an eccentric, rich aristocrat, so when I got my student summer job at Kidlington orange juice factory I was more than a little surprised to see him there in Wellington boots and a hair net, lugging boxes of oranges around. It was then I realised he was just another insecure soul, hiding behind the façade of the university image.

The High Street (or The High)

Stretching from Carfax Tower all the way down to the Cherwell by Magdalen bridge, The High has been the central artery of Oxford for many hundreds of years. Charity shops, clothes shops, posh hotels and colleges are all squeezed together along it, and tucked away near the tower lies the covered market, a maze of more traditional stalls and coffee shops. This market once took pride of place outside on The High up until the 1760s, when, to make the road safer and less congested, it was moved inside. Even back then it seems that traffic on the High Street was a bone of contention.

On May morning, the High is a scene of carnage and chaos as the whole of the town gets up at 5am and tries to squeeze down it to hear the choir sing from the top of Magdalen tower. Then, by about 7am they naturally feel like a pint or three and the pubs open their doors to an onslaught of boozers, happy in the knowledge that last orders is sixteen hours away.

With six colleges directly on the High Street and a further nine clustered close by, this is one of the most important streets in the town for the students and in May and June you'll see them dressed in their official gowns coming here for exams.

After their final paper the students celebrate by drinking champagne and throwing things at each other. It's amusing to watch but best to stand at a discrete distance or you may get caught in the crossfire.

Like many other streets in Oxford, The High has plenty of interesting gargoyles but its strangest must be the one tucked away high up in the corner of Brasenose College, facing St Mary's Church and opposite Oriel Street. Amongst the grotesque figures and weird creatures up there is a little man who appears to be squatting down about to evacuate his bowels. He is in fact doing just this and is a cruel caricature of the foremen in charge of the building site here back in 1886. The builders who erected this part of Brasenose hated him so much that this was their best way of revenge.

Merton Street

Step off The High down one of its many side streets and you will find yourself in one of the most beautiful parts of Oxford. Merton Street has remained relatively unspoiled for centuries with no shops to lure locals, few cars to pollute it and over the years its main inhabitants are still just students and clued-up tourists. Not only is this wide, dreamy cobbled street strung together with beautiful architecture but pass down it and you'll get occasional scintillating glimpses of Christ Church Meadow, just behind Merton and Corpus Christi, which can be reached from Merton Grove.

Merton Street is also home to England's second oldest tennis court, and was used by Charles I in the 1640s when he narrowly lost to Cromwell, 7 sets to 5.

One of the lanes which connects Merton Street with The High used to have the rather outrageous title of 'Grope Cunt Lane', which took its name from having once been part of Oxford's brothel area. The name was toned down later to Grope Street which still caused some hilarity, so it was tamed further still to Grove Street. Finally by some spectacularly surreal leap of the imagination the council changed it to Magpie Lane.

The Eagle and Child on St Giles

St Giles

This wide road begins just by the Ashmolean Museum, eventually splitting into the Woodstock Road and the Banbury Road. Its most recognised feature is the Martyrs Memorial which, like Carfax tower, is a useful reference point and any time of day and night seems to be home to 15 or so foreign students waiting for their guide to show up and take them all to McDonalds.

Although the memorial is a shrine to the three Protestants who were burned at the stake in Broad Street, one summer a group of cheeky students doing tour guides, managed to convince the tourists that it was the remains of a sunken church from when Oxford suffered an earthquake. Continue down St Giles and you'll pass St John's College on your right with its huge gardens and further down two of Oxford's most celebrated pubs, the Lamb and Flag and Eagle and Child, face each other across this busy road, waiting for you with open arms.

Bulwark's Lane

Connecting St Ebbes to George Street, this little-known alleyway is worth seeking out, as it seems to have been all but forgotten by the town. Even at weekends you can follow its windy cobbled path and barely see a soul. Not only does it make a great alternative to battling through

Cornmarket, but with its high stone walls and old gaslights you might feel that by some strange magic you've been transported into some Dickensian mystery rather than out looking for some new pants.

George Street

With its theatres, cinemas, restaurants, chain pubs and clubs you could be led to believing this is Oxford's answer to the West End. Well maybe it is, but with the exception of the Apollo Theatre it could also pass for Doncaster High Street. You will not find the true spirit of Oxford down George Street but you might find a Pizza Hut, some crap pubs and at night-time, if you're lucky, get to see a fight.

CARNIVAL ON BROAD STREET

JERICHO

Somewhat tucked away from the main tourist attractions, Jericho is an area of Oxford that doesn't suffer the usual hoards of visitors yet has plenty to offer and is unusual enough to have earned itself a slightly bohemian reputation.

Its name may have derived from its original remoteness from the city, while some claim it is from the Jericho Gardens which once stood west of the infirmary. Others believe it is named after the Jerry builders who constructed the houses here, which of course begs the question, what is a Jerry builder in the first place?

To get a good feel for the area, take a walk down Walton Street where you'll find cocktail bars, an art-house cinema and a multitude of curious shops selling everything from glow-in-the-dark geese to Art-Deco furniture. Its two most impressive buildings can be found down Walton Street too. The Oxford University Press looks more grandiose than a few colleges I could mention, while Freuds, a popular place for cocktails and food, looks like a cross between the Acropolis and a garden shed.

Round the corner from Freuds lies Little Clarendon Street where suddenly Oxford turns all Mediterranean, with many of its cafés spilling out onto the streets in summer, while at the top, George and Davis' ice-cream parlour serves every flavour you can think of, from

The Jericho Tavern

To some people, Jericho will always be remembered for the Jericho Tavern. This legendary venue was once at the centre of Oxford's music scene, and host to hundreds of bands over many years. Some, like Supergrass, went on to play in huge venues, others, like the Nicotines, are dead and buried. Others still, such as Arthur Turner's Lovechild, have soldiered on despite frequent local petitions to the contrary. Although the venue's demise and tragic conversion to the Fridge-Magnet and Firkin sent the bands and musicians off to Cowley Road, the old room above the pub looks set to be host to local bands again very soon.

mango to chicken and chips.

If you just fancy escaping from it all however, take one of the slip roads past the Oxford University Press building and you'll find yourself down by the Oxford canal, or, if it's wet and slippy, possibly in it. Here you can meet Oxford's barge community (you can't miss them, they all wear wellies and sport beards) and either wander along the path back into town or lose yourself out towards Banbury.

A cocktail at Freuds, a meal at Al Shami, a movie at the Phoenix or a pint in Jude the Obscure, Jericho is also a place where you could spend a perfect evening in Oxford. Oh my god I'm beginning to sound like an advert for local radio…

Jericho as seen through the eyes of local artist Al Cane

THE COWLEY ROAD

Starting just past Magdalen bridge and sitting between Iffley Road and St Clement's lies Oxford's most improbable street. Something of the black sheep of the family, Cowley Road may be dirty and ugly compared to the rest of Oxford, but its diversity and spirit make it very much the cosmopolitan hub of the city.

A walk up Cowley Road and Oxford suddenly transforms into a wonderful mix of curry houses, health food stores, halal meat shops, exotic clothes shops, squats, sex shops, great pubs, health clinics and of course Fred's Discount Store which, until recently, sold a range of basic household utilities together with cheap erotic underwear.

At night Cowley Road thrives and some of Oxford's best pubs can be found here. The New Inn, in all its squalid glory, is still a popular hang-out for musicians, the Elm Tree is a pub

that seems in a state of permanent blissful drunkenness, the Temple Bar is just terrific and the two designer bars at the top of the Cowley Road add some glamour, despite looking a bit at odds amongst the greasy spoon cafés and kebab shops.

One of Oxford's most important clubs, the Zodiac is here, which pulls big crowds at the weekends, as do the Bullingdon Arms and the Point, so it's no surprise that Oxford's music scene should be focused here too. In fact all the big name bands have lived in the Cowley Road area at some point in their career, and the likes of Mark Gardner and Danny from Supergrass can still be spotted around. Even Radiohead all lived together at 5 Ridgefield Road back in 1991 to focus on their songwriting, until constant arguments turned the house into a mini version of Lord of the Flies, culminating in Colin the bass player being tied up and tortured by the rest of the band for not doing the washing up.

The Strange Ones

Immortalised in the Supergrass song 'The Strange Ones', Cowley Road is home to many of Oxford's drunks, druggies, down-and-outs and eccentrics. Walk down the street any time of day or night and chances are that someone will try and sell you an oxo cube masquerading as dope, you'll nearly be knocked over as a man hurtles by in a Tesco's shopping trolley and you might even see the Scottish guy with the bone through his nose. Stories about this place and its strange and often disturbed inhabitants are numerous but rarely exaggerated.

A friend of mine tells of her first day in Oxford when she took a stroll down the Cowley Road and was surprised to see a barefooted man walk past her talking loudly to himself and wearing what appeared to be a carpet. Moments later a woman carrying a plank of wood came running up the street shouting 'Bob, Bob, Bob!!!'

She finally met up with Bob, who was an old drunk guy in a wheelchair and when she reached him she stood there panting for a few seconds. Then, when she'd got her breath back, she started hitting him repeatedly over the head with the plank of wood…

I too remember the summer I came to live here, a man appeared on the corner of Magdalen Road sat in a plush velvet chair with another empty chair next to him. After a couple of days of his continued presence I plucked up the courage to ask him what he was doing.

''Street philosophy my friend….' he said in a thick, sad Eastern European accent and beckoned me to sit in the chair next to him.

'…for only 50p I will tell you why your life is a string of meaningless episodes of suffering.'

Although I declined his kind offer I had been inaugurated into the Cowley Road.

Why is Cowley Road so weird, what is the magic triangle and where can I buy Mr. T slippers?

The area's full correct name of Temple Cowley has led some occultists to conclude this land may once have been owned by the mystical sect of the Knights Templar, which would have made the land holy, blessed and magical, which, with all those kebab shops, it clearly isn't.

New Age legend also decrees that powerful ley-lines run down Cowley Road and Iffley Road (hence the names Cow-ley and Iff-ley) converging at the sweet counter of Bottoms Up by Magdalen bridge. This may help explain why Cowley Road is unusual but in turn fails to explain why Iffley Road is so dull in comparison. Live in this area for more than a year, the legend continues, and everyone you come to know will live within it too, your love-life will blossom here, you won't be able to leave for less than five years and you will develop a fondness for Easy-Listening music.

The Cowley triangle is capped by Magdalen Road which is also a spiritual mecca in its own right. Not only is it home to the Inner Bookshop and Magic Café, (the focal point of Oxford's hippie and occultist community) but you'll also find a Buddhist temple, a nunnery, sharks and piranhas at the Goldfish Bowl and one of my favourite places, Sylvester's. Not really existing in the universe as we know it, Sylvester's is a cross between Dr Who's Tardis and the local shop in the League of Gentlemen. This is the shop from magical childhood stories and they seem to stock everything your imagination could conjure up, from Roland Rat tea towels to fake moss.

A typical Cowley Road resident

Cowley Rhododendrums
Number 30 Henley Street

Although its hey-day has been and gone and it's all a bit run-down nowadays, this garden is still a strange spectacle to behold. A breeze-block fortress with a doll's head in one of the turrets sits among other bizarre items while half-hidden behind the ivy (that threatens to topple the house over) sits a two-foot high shrine with a figure inside. Elsewhere in the ivy an over-sized owl stares down into the pond that once lit up. Very David Lynch, very scary. Visit at night. Alone.

43 Magdalen Road

Looking like an Amazonian rainforest in the summer, with its strange collection of toys and artefacts lying around, you should even spot Charles Dickens skulking in the bushes. Inside is even better and guided tours might be on the agenda next year.

HEADINGTON

Follow St Clement's and Headington Road up the hill and you'll find this area, home to Oxford football grounds, the shark house and one-time home to writer JRR Tolkein and crooked businessman Robert Maxwell.

Headington is little more than a residential part of Oxford and apart from visiting the shark you'd be unlikely to want to stick around too long, although the Old Village and Bury Knowle Park just after the lights can be quite pleasant for a wander round. If you are up in the area, Café Noir does some pretty good French cuisine, and for bargain-seekers Headington is a good place to come for an afternoon's charity shop crawl, as there are at least five or six of them here. If you're looking for any more excitement….forget it.

Even parking punts in Oxford is a nightmare

PARKS AND GARDENS

Compared to most cities, Oxford has an enviable selection of parks and gardens. You can be just about anywhere in the city and a vast meadow and riverside walk is waiting just around the corner to take you away from the traffic and crowds. Add to that the lawns and gardens of the different colleges and it's easy to see why Oxford is so cherished for its greenery.

Christ Church Meadow
Open 7am-dusk
Entered off St Aldates through the War Memorial Gardens

This beautiful meadow lying in the very heart of Oxford is not only a haven away from the noise of the city but is also the home to a rather unlikely herd of long-haired cows which have grazed here for centuries. Pass through the War Memorial and the central pathway (known as Broad Walk) and this will take you right up to the river where the back of the Botanic Gardens, St Hildas and the top of Magdalen tower can all be seen. Take the path round to the right and you can follow the river on its winding trail away from the town. Parallel to Broad Walk and flanking the back of Christ Church and Merton College is the pathway known as Dead Man's Walk. This was the original path trod by Oxford's Jewish community many centuries ago to carry their dead from the nearby synagogue to the Jewish burial ground, now the location of the Botanical Gardens. Anti-semitism was the

The gates of St John's College

reason for this special route, as Jews were not permitted to take their dead through the city-centre. Nowadays it is steeped in legends and ghost stories, probably springing more from its evocative name than anything else.

South Park

Found at the top of St Clement's on the right

Renowned for its majestic view of the dreamy spires, (if you ignore the cranes and telegraph wires in the background) this park is found just up St Clement's and creeps up the hill all the way to Brookes University. It has plenty of space for football matches (including a few marked pitches), a few good climbing trees and a rather dilapidated fitness trail in the top corner. Throughout May to August it is host to the council organised Party in the Park events when it is transformed with firework displays, bands, fairground rides and lantern processions.

Headington Hill Park

Found at the top of St Clement's, on the left, opposite South Park

One of Oxford's best-kept secrets, this secluded park, just past Magdalen bridge, is one of the most peaceful of the city's many green areas. While its neighbour, South Park, is little more than a big field for football games, Headington Hill is the perfect park for a romantic stroll or some quiet introspection. Especially beautiful in spring when the trees blossom, huge carpets of daisies cover the ground and a host of friendly squirrels turn it into a Walt Disney cartoon.

University Parks

Parks Road Open 8am to dusk

Centrally located and partly-encircled by university buildings, this 100 acre park lives up to its name, being a popular spot for student joggers and the University Cricket Team to practice in, while the more sensible students can be found idling their time here over a bottle of Pimms.

Despite its popularity it is still possible to lose yourself in the park grounds. Walk all the way to the back and the orderly array of mown lawns, flower beds and fir trees give way to a wild meadow over the river Cherwell and the chance for an idyllic riverside walk.

The Botanic Gardens

By Magdalen Bridge on the High Street (01865) 276920
April-Sept Open 9am-5pm
Greenhouses open 10am-4.30pm
Oct-March open 9am-4.30pm
Greenhouses open 10am-4pm
£2 admission

Built on the site of the old Jewish burial ground, the Botanic Gardens were originally set up for the cultivation of medicinal herbs in the 17th century, but have since grown to become one of the country's most diverse collection of plants.

The outdoor gardens, although hardly outstanding, are pleasant enough to wander round any time of year and there's a short clockwise walk you can do past the river and the bog garden which will bring you back to the entrance. With so many rich green areas in Oxford you might wonder why anyone would want to pay to come here, but the feature that helps to make the Botanic Garden so popular is its greenhouses.

Rather than tomatoes and runner beans, you'll find all sorts of exotic plants here, with each greenhouse having its own special type of plants and its own unique smell. Look out for the giant oil palm and the cacti room full of enormous prickly characters and carnivorous plants. The greenhouse with the pond and big lily pads also has these tiny fish that nibble your fingernails when you put your hands in the water (though they didn't seem that interested last time I was here).

Worth looking out for too is the Black Border, located outside the orchids greenhouse and facing the river. This strange collection of different black plants looks altogether alien amongst all the greenery of the garden.

And finally after exiting, don't miss the Midgets' Maze at the front of the building, just before you re-join the High Street. This was constructed in the late 18th century for the dwarf children of the Dean of Magdalen and has been kept in perfect condition ever since their tiny ghosts were spotted playing here over 100 years ago by one of the gardeners.

Punting in University Parks

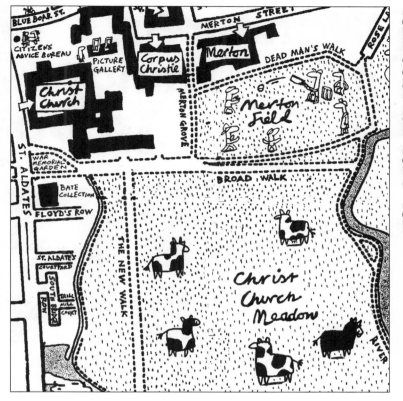

Wonderful Things To Do

MUSEUMS

The Ashmolean Museum
Beaumont Street (01865) 278000
www.asmol.ox.ac.uk
Open Tues-Sat 10am-5pm Sun 2pm-5pm free

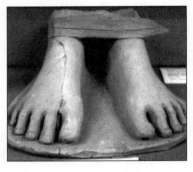

Once a Roman brothel, this renowned museum is now home to three floors of innumerable pots, coins, paintings, statues, jewellery and Europe's largest collection of Tupperware. The building itself is beautiful but as a museum suffers badly from being old-fashioned. Most things are stuck in glass cabinets or on the wall, and with no interactive facilities and very little in the way of information about them, after a while you couldn't care less whether the vase you're looking at is Grecian, Ming or Ikea.

To make the most out of the museum, I recommend talking to the curators, found dotted around the place. This may seem a bit daunting, but if you feed them a few nibbles, (Rich Tea biscuits and pepperami seem to go down well) they'll tell you some good stories about the different items in each room and make your visit infinitely more enjoyable. June Cable is particularly good value for money. Not only does she tell good anecdotes about the museum items but she'll also tell you stories about her regular trips to Transylvania, and how to contact the afterlife.

On the ground floor, the Egyptian section is worth a look around, boasting a few good mummies, as is the Indian gallery with its collection of Krishna, Buddha and Siva Parvati statues.

Up on the first and second floor there are loads of paintings, mainly revolving around the themes of fruit, vegetables, Christianity and dead ducks. One notable highlight however is room 38 for its painting – 'Big nose and shells' which can be viewed from the special seating area.

Other highlights include:
- Guy Fawkes' lantern in room 27
- The mummified hand in room 28
- The Alfred Jewel in the Leeds gallery 1st floor
- The Stradivarius in the music room.

(Reputed to be the best and most famous violin in the world. It is in a protected glass cabinet, but if you put down a 50p deposit, they'll let you have a go on it)

On weekdays you will invariably find yourself surrounded by parties of school children running around doing South Park impressions in the Egyptian and Greek rooms. At weekends you will find yourself engulfed by impenetrable crowds of foreign students with novelty sheep rucksacks. Choose your own nightmare.

A cheeky tale

The last time I was in the Ashmoleon with Dippy, we were passing one of the old curators engrossed in her crossword when Dippy chose that moment to drop a silent stinker. Without even looking up she calmly pulled out a can of air freshener from her bag, sprayed it in Dippy's direction and immediately returned to her crossword, not a flicker of emotion on her face. A true professional.

The Stolen Cézanne

The dawning of the new millenium was predicted as triggering mass cult suicides, the terrible bug and the end of Céline Dion* but the only extraordinary event to happen on New Year's Eve occured right here in Oxford.

In a style straight out of Pink Panther movies, two guys came through the skyline into the Impressionists gallery and set off smoke bombs. While the guards went to call the fire brigade the thieves helped themselves to the Cézanne painting 'Auvres-sur-Oise'. In the room were other paintings by the likes of Picasso and Monet, which mysteriously were left alone. Police figure this to be the work of two men: one an art lover and the other a renowned criminal and have recently released these crude photo fits.

*she made a pledge on TV to give up singing in the New Year but this seemed to be somewhat akin to Status Quo's farewell gig back in 1986.

Bates Collection of Musical Instruments Faculty of Music

St Aldates (01865) 276139
www.asmol.ox.ac.uk/bcmi-page.html
Open Mon-Fri 2pm-5pm Sat 10am-12pm free

From Alpine horns to harpsichords and the peculiar serpent, this is a small but varied collection of Western classical instruments from the last few hundred years. Nothing can be played or touched except the Muselaar (a sort of harpsichord) which, thanks to the over-zealous hands of small children, has missing and out of tune notes, but still makes a gorgeous sound. To be honest, the place is really only of interest to musicians or lovers of antique objects. If you bring kids, get them to look out for Bertie the bat.

Curioxity

Old Fire Station 40 George Street (01865) 247004
Open weekends, half terms and school holidays 10am-4pm
Kids £1.80 Adults £2.10

I found this place akin to one of the lower levels of Dante's Inferno as I chose half term to review it and discovered it to be it unbearably hot, stuffy, packed with ankle-biters and they wouldn't even let me smoke in there.

But, if you've got kids they'll love the place. It's all hands-on science stuff with two-way mirrors, optical illusions and other gizmos. The price seems a bit steep for what it is but your children will have great fun for an hour. The challenge, as with all kids, is to see how quickly they can break the child-proof exhibits.

Museum of Modern Art (MOMA)

30 Pembroke Street (01865) 7227733
Open Tues-Sat 11am-6pm Thurs 11am-9pm Sun 2pm-6pm £2.50 /£1.50 Free Thurs 6pm-9pm

Perfectly-sized gallery space offering everything from photo exhibitions to installations. This myriad of white rooms is the ideal setting for seeing everything from Yoko Ono's latest to a Robert Doisneau retrospective. I've yet to be disappointed with any exhibition I've seen here.

Oxford University Press Museum

Tour arranged by appointment only, up to groups of four during office hours, sometimes in the evenings if they're feeling nice. Admission Free
Tel Martin Maw (01865) 556767

Modelled on the arch of Constantine, the University Press building in Jericho is more impressive than some of the University buildings I could mention.

The museum is housed in one of the rooms here and I must admit, after a brief look at the place, I thought I was going to find it pretty dull. But Jennifer who showed me round made me glad I'd visited as she told a few good stories about the place and made it all pretty interesting.

The exhibits are kept in one room and you're basically taken on a half-hour tour with anecdotes about each exhibit from early printing devices right up to the Biggles books.

Once past the 1920s hot metal printing photo, (look for Douglas Hurd sat in the centre) the story becomes particularly interesting with the introduction of a character called James Murray. This heavily bearded brain-box, who looked like Grandad from Only Fools and Horses, decided once and for all to fullfill his childhood dream and compile a dictionary in his shed with the help of, amongst other people, convicted murderer Dr Minor. The story is currently being made into a feature film so I won't spoil the plot but, needless to say, it's a happy ending as the Oxford English Dictionary is now the definitive dictionary world-wide.

If you want to do your bit for the development of the English language, find a new word that isn't in the dictionary, send 4 examples of it in print to these guys and it should appear in the next update.

Online submission form www.oed.com

The Tennis Courts
Merton Street
Admission 50p

Tennis enthusiasts might be interested to know that this is one of only a handful of 19th century tennis courts in existence, done out in its original colours of red and black, and still being used. Charles I used these courts to exercise in during the siege of Oxford in the 1640s. To find it, wander halfway down the cobbled part of Merton Street and you should notice the tennis shop on the side of the road closest to the High Street. If you're not a sports fanatic you might find your 50p better spent on chocolate.

The University Museum of Natural History
Parks Road opposite Keble College
(01865) 270949
www.ashmol.ox.ac.uk/oum
Open Mon-Sat 12am-5pm Free

This unassuming museum found next to University Parks is like some great adventurer sat by the fire with his pipe and slippers who welcomes you in and waves around in an ambiguous way saying -

'Oh it's nothing really, just a little something I collected when I was in Peru…' before returning to his Sunday crossword.

Don't be put off by its modesty. From the moment you enter, you may notice the stink of mothballs but more importantly you'll realise how beautiful this building is, with its dazzling array of zoological exhibits, swimming in light from its high glass ceiling.

The place is filled with skeletons, stuffed animals, minerals and dinosaur footprints; in fact, the only living things in here are a colony of bees half way up the stairs and one or two of the curators.

The skeletons are of course mightily impressive and the building is home to everything from rodents to elephants and giant fish, not to mention the cast of an Iguanadon. As well as a fascinating and well-presented selection of natural history they also have various on-going photographic exhibitions on display, many of which have been fantastic.

After you've finished marvelling at it all and found the Dodo, take the stairs up to the balcony and you'll be rewarded with a great view of the building as well as being scrutinised by half of the UK's bird population from behind glass cabinets. Look out also for the sun, moon and earth up there.

The Darwinian Debate of 1860

The University Museum is well known for having housed the legendary Darwinian debate that romantic scientists (if they exist) hold as a moment of great triumph over Christianity. The story goes that in the library many eminent men were present including scientist TH Huxley and William Wilberforce, the bishop of Oxford.

As the debate got more heated the Bishop finally stood up and said: *'So tell me Mr Huxley, is it your grandfather's or grandmother's side which is descended from a monkey?'*

Amid laughter Huxley instantly replied: *'I'd rather be descended from a monkey than from a bishop like Wilberforce.'*

What we learn from this however is not that science triumphed over religion but that even the most intelligent people in the heat of a discussion will resort to arguments like *'My dad's better than your dad.'*

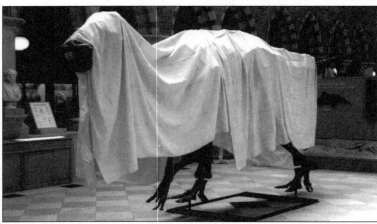

Sporting the latest in Dinosaur fashion

Science Museum
Closed until October 2001 when they should have a new foundation.

(For other museums see Weird Section).

WHERE TO GET HIGH

St Mary's Tower
High Street Admission £1.60 adults

While the final ascent up an impossibly narrow spiral staircase is not for the faint-hearted, this is definitely the best of the 'stunning views of Oxford' on offer. Not only are the panoramic sights magnificent, this is also the highest you can get in Oxford without parting with £16 quid on the Cowley Road. The view takes in the 4 corners of Oxford, most notably looking down over the Radcliffe Camera and the mysteriously quiet All Souls College, as well as Brasenose, Lincoln and Exeter.

Try your best to visit off-season, or if you can't, first thing in the morning, as waiting half an hour in the heat for a busload of Japanese tourists to descend the staircase may well taint your experience. Whilst up there you should see that the whole of the spire is decorated in what looks like stone tulips, though I could be wildly off the mark here. Plus, if you look carefully in each corner, you can throw a coin onto the back of a gargoyle and make a wish. If you miss, hope that no-one is standing underneath. If they are, hide.

A Brief History
Historically, the church and its tower date back as far as the 14th century when this humble little church was actually at the very centre of student life. Renowned men of Oxford were buried here, such as John Radcliffe and John Wesley and the church has been used for everything from examinations, ceremonies and lectures to executions. Being an expert in Baroque architecture I couldn't let you visit St Mary's without asking you to look out for the south porch of the church. With its impressive lattice columns modelled on St Peter's in Rome, it cuts a fine figure for itself on the High Street.

Incidentally, just because there are loads of graffiti up there doesn't mean it's an open invitation for all and sundry to join in. I watched incredulously last year as a respectable looking Italian man in his late fifties (accompanied by his equally well-groomed wife) pulled a pen out of his pocket, nonchalantly scribbled his name on the wall and then went back to licking his ice-cream.

All Souls College as seen by a very tall man

Carfax Tower

Top of the High Street
Open April-Oct 10am-5.30pm,
Nov-March 10am-3.30pm
Closed 25th Dec-1st Jan
Adult £1.20 Child 60p No under 5's

Probably the most useful building to know if you're new to Oxford, as it will invariably crop up when needing directions to somewhere in the town centre. The tower is the only remains of a 13th century church, and the name Carfax comes from the Latin 'Quadri furcus', an ancient pizza topping meaning four mushrooms and referring to the shape of the church's four enormous bells. You get to climb the 99 steps of the tight winding spiral staircase to the top for the awesome view of the town.

Once at the top, it's definitely worth having a look through the free telescope. Although it says 20p, it's been broken for years, and despite it being really tricky to get a coin in, it still manages to take about £200 a year.

When you've finished enjoying the views and taken way too many photos, look out for Oxford's most surreal graffiti –

'we bow to Kaboola, god of cheese'.
And finally on the way down look for the crucified rabbit in the cabinet.

During high season it can be ridiculously busy, and uncomfortably claustrophic. To avoid the crowds come early in the morning or stick on your Spiderman outfit and try scaling the outside.

A Brief History

By 1032, St Martin's Church (now Carfax) stood at the town centre's main crossroad and entered history as the spot where the infamous Town and Gown riots took place in 1355.

A lesser known fact about Carfax tower is the existence of a child's grave on the way in, just under the chair on the left. In fact the old graveyard of this church still lies below the café next door but it's probably best not to tell them.

oohh…   *…ahhhh…*

The four stunning views of Oxford from Carfax Tower

…mmm…   *…eurgh.*

The Sheldonian Theatre

Broad Street Open 10am-12.30pm
2pm-4pm most days Admission £1.50

Built in the late 1600s by Sir Christopher Wren, the Sheldonian's name and design have Roman origins and for many centuries it was used principally for ceremonial purposes. Nowadays it is still used by the colleges for degree-giving ceremonies but is used much more for music events. You won't see Oasis in here, but everything from Beethoven to Cleo Lane will get put on *'as long as they're in keeping with the building and don't wreck it'*. Its high painted ceiling is said to depict 'Truth combined with the Arts and Sciences, to expel ignorance from the University'. A task successfully achieved with the exception of one or two students from Christ Church. For your money you also get to climb to the cupola at the top for a panoramic view of Oxford which gives a good opportunity for some gargoyle spotting.

Personally, I'd recommend saving your money and experiencing the Sheldonian properly by coming to a concert, but, if that's not possible it's worth a visit, especially if you're around in June for Encaenia. This is the one time when all the top nobs from the universities get dressed up and parade through the town to the theatre where they deliver honourary degrees to anyone with a fat enough cheque book.

Life for the students at Oxford begins and ends at the Sheldonian Theatre. In the second week of the first term everyone dresses up in Sub Fuse* for matriculation and then after a ten minute speech in Latin (which no-one understands) they are official students of Oxford and everyone celebrates with a glass of fizzy pop. Life at the University ends with Graduation, although this has to be booked by each student separately and I have heard nightmare tales of students waiting up to four years to graduate.

The Radcliffe Camera

Radcliffe Square (no public access)

This magnificent round library was built principally as a glorified reading room for students but over the years has also become an extension of the Bodleian library nearby. Opened in 1749 this has to be one of the most photographed buildings in Oxford but otherwise there is little else of interest about it, unless you're lucky enough to get a glimpse inside, a privilege normally reserved for students and Inspector Morse (whenever a corpse is found in there).

There is a story I heard about one drunken don from Brasenose who was famous for getting so blind drunk at night that he would always have to feel his way along the walls to get back inside his college. Apparently one night he staggered across to the Radcliffe Camera and spent the whole night just going round and round....

*The clobber they wear for exams and graduation

How Francis saved Oxford's bacon

Folly Bridge Tower is the location of a story about how a couple of centuries ago a bunch of cocky Cambridge students came to Oxford intent on proving once and for all that Cambridge undergraduates were intellectually superior.

On arriving at the tower they called up in Latin, expecting to humiliate the simple custodian they imagined would be working there. But the tower's custodian happened to be none other than one of the 13th century's most famous scholars, Roger Bacon, (doing a bit of part-time work on the side) and he naturally replied in fluent Latin. This was enough to intimidate the Cambridge students. If the keeper of the tower could speak fluent Latin, they figured that the Oxford students would probably have mastered the ability to travel backwards in time and how to make the perfect puff-pastry. The story ends with them fleeing back to Cambridge and to this day bacon is still off the menu in most Cambridge colleges.

The Radcliffe Camera

is ridiculously over the top but still much more in keeping with Oxford's architecture than some of the 20th century monstrosities I could mention. Folly Bridge, which it stands on, marks the original Southern entrance to the city and once boasted a magnificent tower which was pulled down in 1779 as part of a traffic calming scheme. If only they had known what they were starting.

The Bridge of Sighs
New college Lane

The bridge is one of the most famous sights in Oxford and is modelled on the famous Venetian bridge that connected to the prison from which Casanova escaped. Built in the late 19th century to link up New College and Hertford, it was blocked up recently when, Hertford's cat, Simpkins, developed a habit of using New College library as his litter tray.

Caudwell's Castle
Folly Bridge St Aldates (no public access)

If you're down St Aldate's look out for this building just on the right hand side of Folly bridge. Built in 1849, this Venetian Palazzo style affair was dreamed up by wealthy eccentric Joshua Caudwell who delighted in surrounding his home with classical statues and cannons. The whole thing

View into the Old School's Quad

of Sighs and is open only to students who can come in and use it like a reference library. Paid tours are organised a few times a day for visitors and will take you around the Duke Humphrey's Library and Divinity School, although the price is a bit steep and it's not that exciting either. It's nice just to wander through here from Radcliffe square or Catte Street and look at the buildings.

Trivia-wise, students still have to take an oath that they won't take sheep inside the building and, according to statistics, each book in the Bodleian library is read approximately once every 16 years.

Oxford Castle
New Road (no public access)
Built around the time of the Norman Conquest, this hasn't fared well against the ravages of time and nowadays is not so much a building as a grassy knoll. Despite it being officially out of bounds to the public, it is still used by snowboarders in winter seeking a cheap thrill and is a popular spot for fornicating students.

The Bodleian Library and Gallery
Old School's Quad (01865) 277000
Open Mon-Sat 9.30pm-4.45pm Free
Built above the Divinity School, this is one of only three copyright libraries in England which receive a free copy of every new book published. The Bodleian library is part of a confusing cluster of buildings that sit in Old School's Quad opposite the Bridge

The Ice Rink
Oxpen's Road
Disfigured in his early teens by an experiment with a chemistry set that went tragically wrong, architect Colin Grote perhaps best described his bitter frustration with the world with the design of this building in 1963. Despite winning many awards, in particular the coveted 'Hurray for Grey' award in Canada in 1968, it has never been to everyone's taste. In the 1980s the building came under the wrath of Prince Charles who described it as *'a corrugated dog-turd with tentacles.'*

Despite this, many other 20th century architects have attempted to emulate Grote's unique style but none have quite matched up to it, although whoever built the Beehive in St John's College had a lot of fun trying.

WHERE TO TAKE A GOOD STROLL

City Centre*

Your mission, should you choose it, is to find Magpie Lane half way down the High Street. Once down this narrow side street you'll be in one of the most unspoiled parts of Oxford; Merton Street. This long cobbled street is home to a cluster of colleges and despite its beauty is relatively unknown by many citizens of Oxford as there are no shops down here, but the lack of pedestrians and cars makes it all the more magical. Continue until you're back to the High, cross the road and to your left head down Queens Lane; another quiet, timeless street. Make sure to look out for a motley collection of gargoyles staring down at you from the high wall of New College on your right, then as you pass the bend you'll

be rewarded with the Bridge of Sighs. Down the alleyway just before it, (once known as Hell Passage) lies the beer-drinkers utopia known as the Turf Tavern, from here most people forget about the walk and concentrate on sampling all the different ales in the pub. If you make it out of the Turf alive, take a left onto Catte street and you'll pass two of Oxford's most famous buildings, the Bodleian Library and the Radcliffe Camera. To finish your walk in style, take a trip up St Mary's Tower at the end of the square for a panoramic view of the city and a chance to get intimate with a group of Japanese tourists in the tight passageways around the top of the tower. Back to earth you'll find you're almost back where you started, tired, wiser and probably a little sozzled.

*See map on page 47

Merton Street

Port Meadow

Port Meadow is a vast stretch of greenery on the edge of Oxford, used for the Oxford horse races in June and best-loved for the walk to the two pubs, the Perch and the Trout, a few miles along the river.

To find it go down Walton Street past the Phoenix cinema, turn left at the small roundabout past Lucy and you'll find the car-park at the bottom of the road.

To get to the Perch go straight across the meadow and once over the bridge turn right. After passing the boat yard it is about twenty minutes walk along from here.

For the more adventurous, the Trout is another couple of miles along the river and not only is it a better pub but the walk gets more pleasant from here too. Continue along and the path will widen out with more meadowland and trees on your left. Once over the lock you're almost there and if it's after 12pm you've only a short two-hour wait before you eat.

(See Watering Holes for reviews of these two pubs)

St Aldate's River Walk

Down St Aldates, past the Head of the River pub, you'll find a path on your left leading to the river just after the cruise boats. This path meanders its way along the Isis all the way to Donnington Bridge passing some lovely countryside, resident swans and the myriad of rowing establishments. During term time you might be lucky to catch the University rowing teams out with the coxes who cycle along following the rowers shouting insulting remarks to make them go faster.

When you reach Donnington Bridge take a left and Iffley Road will take you back into town or turn right to reach Abingdon Road. Continue along under the bridge, however, and you'll reach the Isis Tavern where lunch or a shifty pint awaits.

A word of warning, if it rained recently this can be a relentless nightmare of puddles and mud. Stick on your wellies and hope for the best.

Canal Walk Jericho

Starting at the upper end of Hythe Bridge Street and continuing all the way to the bridge on Walton Well Road, this is a twenty minute stroll along Oxford's canal taking in the barge community, plenty of greenery and a few ducks. To know where to leave the trail, look for the red brick bridge (you'll know you've got there as the walk tails off with the arrival of an ugly dilapidated building on your right). Turn right at the bridge and you'll be back on Walton Street where it's only a short walk into the town centre, though I recommend stopping at the Jericho café for a bite to eat.

For the more adventurous, the canal walk does continue all the way to Banbury but it might take you a day or two to get there.

Iffley Village and Lock

Iffley village, engulfed by the ever-expanding town of Oxford many years ago, and once threatened with being squashed under Stevenson's railway track, somehow managed to survive. What's more it has withstood the ravages of change to remain an eerily quiet village on the outskirts of Oxford. To get there follow the Iffley Road from town and once you're past the Donnington Bridge lights, take the second right. From here cross the small roundabout and you'll find yourself in this beautiful village. Wander along Church Way and you'll pass The Prince of Wales, which is worth noting as it does one

of the best pub lunches in Oxford. On reaching Mill Lane on your right, follow this down to the end, go through the narrow sheltered walkway and then over the lock with the water crashing below you. I've done this walk every time of year from the coldest winter night, when your breath hangs frozen in the air, to the warmest summer morning and it always brings a flood of happiness whenever I'm down there.

Once over the mathematical bridge, to your left is the meadow supporting one of England's rarest flowers: the Snakeshead Fritillaries, to the right is the path along the lock to the Isis Tavern. If you continue on this path along the river for long enough it'll take you into the heart of the town and curiously you'll be at the start of the St Aldate's river walk.

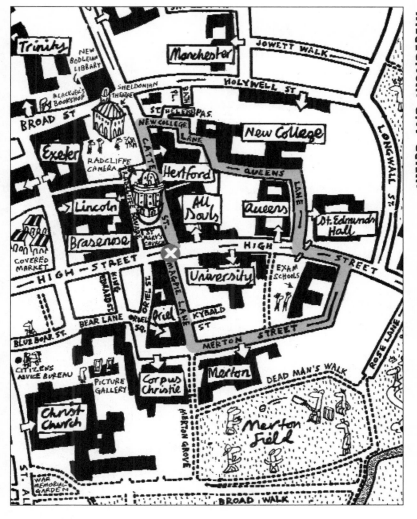

CITY CENTRE WALK
Start at the cross and follow the grey path anti-clockwise.

PUNTING

One of the most wonderful and frustrating activities to undertake in Oxford. Be very careful not to underestimate the complexity involved in moving a boat with a pole between point A & B. Invariably, you will also visit points D, E and Y, but you will have learned something along the way.

Oxford provides a number of locations to begin your adventure, all of which allow you to explore different parts of the river and also various drinking houses during you trip. Be aware of the long traditions associated with the sport. The most famous is the punter's standing position on the punt. In Oxford we stand on the curved, rough end, while in Cambridge they stand on the smooth, flat end. In weighing up the pros and cons of each method, the Oxford approach is, of course, by far the most economical and attractive method.

HOW TO PUNT

1) Get onto your boat by using both of your legs.
2) Stand on the curved end of the punt.
3) Check there are no splinters along the pole. If there are, remove them and sand down the remaining surface.
4) Never try and get more than five or six people in a punt. Over thirty is really asking for trouble.
5) Look confident and don't slouch.
6) Push away from riverbank.
7) To go forward, keep the pole tight to the boat at a sharp angle facing away from the punt.
8) Raise pole to full extension and drop through hands into water until contact is made with the bottom of river.
9) Use the pole as a rudder to steer out of the way of oncoming vehicles and large ducks (some of which have been measured at two metres in length and have been known to wrestle unwary punters to their watery grave).
10) Remember, you have to get back to where you started, so don't be too ambitious in your journey, London is further than you think.
11) Watch out for bridges as you have a very long pole in your hand and it points straight up in the air.
12) Whatever you do, never hold onto the pole when it gets stuck into the mud. It is better to lose the pole than your hard-earned integrity.

FIGHTING TECHNIQUES

When ramming another punt, aim for the standing punter. The pole can be used to hit the opponent's ankles but remember to keep low at the moment of attack.

Do:

1) Bring booze. Pimms and fizzy white wine are very popular.
2) Go when it's sunny.
3) Swing from low branches as you pass beneath them.
4) Be careful of large boats when punting on the Thames.
5) Take water pistols.
6) Take sun tan cream and waterproofs.

Don't:

1) Bring any pets, especially Dulux dogs, large members of the cat family, or horses.
2) Attempt punting when under the influence of strong hallucinogenics.
3) Rock the boat (unless copulating).
4) Bring any high voltage equipment on the punt with you.
5) Drink from the river, unless you collect unusual skin complaints.

PUNTING COMPANIES

Cherwell Boathouse

To find it go along the Banbury Road, right into Bardwell Street and watch out for signs. £8-10 per hour. £40-50 all day. Deposit – one day's hire. Available 10am-7pm. Mid March-Mid Oct. (01865) 515978

The main advantage of coming here is the lack of powered vehicles on this stretch of the river and the wealth of places to eat at nearby. The Boathouse is an excellent but pricey restaurant, while about an hour upstream is the Victoria Arms, which has a docking station, play area and is open all day with lunchtime pub grub, (01865) 241382, food from 12pm-2.30pm. Downstream, the University Parks is excellent for picnics and a bit further is Parsons Pleasure, once a nude sunbathing area used by University dons and now a family-friendly Naturists picnic area.

Magdalen Bridge

Old Horse Ford, underneath the bridge. (01865) 202643 £9-£10 per hour. £25 deposit and ID required.

This place has been operating for over 100 years now and is a great starting point for drifting down past the Botanic Gardens and beyond to Christ Church Meadow. If you continue you can reach the Head of the River pub for refreshments and a chance to be photographed by a party of foreign students. You can also organise chauffeured punts from Magdalen Bridge, it's pretty expensive but you do get free fizzy white wine.

There are also two more punting spots to be found next to The Head Of The River pub on St Aldate's.

Weird Things To Do

UNDER-GRADS   POST-GRADS

The Pitt River's Museum

Behind the Natural History Museum,
Parks Road (01865) 270927
Open 11am-4.30 pm Mon-Sat 12pm-
4.30pm Sun www.prm.ox.ac.uk

If I had to pick out my favourite thing
in Oxford it would be this. The Pitt
River's Museum is nothing less than a
mysterious and frightening collection
of ethnological curiosities. If Indiana
Jones, Aleister Crowley and Joseph
Campbell had got together to create
a museum, this would be it. Housed
at the back of the University Museum
of Natural History, the Pitt River's has
three floors of artefacts all crammed
into wonderfully decrepit glass
cabinets. What the top floor lacks in
interest with its collection of
weaponry, the ground and first floor
compensate for, with everything from
a 40 foot totem pole to shrunken
heads, voodoo dolls and witchcraft
charms. With its gloomy lighting,
some corners of the museum are so
dark that the curators carry torches
around to help visitors read the tiny
hand-written labels that accompany
the artifacts, but of course this only
adds to the museum's peculiar charm.
Trying to locate things is another

difficulty because, despite the cabinets
being numbered, the figures are so
discrete that they are almost
impossible to find. See something
really weird and five minutes later you
might never be able to find it again.

Many visitors to the museum fail
to see the drawers that sit underneath
the display cabinets, which is a shame.
There are literally hundreds dotted
around the place and being (naturally)
unlabelled you might open one up to
find a mummified toad, open another
and a severed finger points back at
you accusingly.

Did I really see an eyeball in a jar last time I was here, I could have sworn it was in this cabinet?...

As you enter on the ground floor you shouldn't find it too difficult to discover the museum's most talked about exhibits; the shrunken heads. This cabinet, 'head-hunter's trophies,' with its gruesome heads, skulls and scalps is found underneath the boat hanging from the ceiling, and usually has a crowd around it. Nearby, the 'treatment of the dead' cabinet has a tiny jar with a baby foetus in it.

Down the right-hand wall lies the mummy with her little toe sticking out from the bandages (said to wiggle on her birthday) and the weird looking nail man. Opposite them lies the 'Sympathetic Magic' section under which the drawers contain some of the museum's best-kept secrets. Look in the top middle drawer and you'll find a beeswax voodoo doll with pins

Other oddities
(if you can find them)

GROUND FLOOR
Ballerina flies
Made with head and thorax of a large fly (case 145)
The Hawaiian feather coat
Far left-hand corner, look for the curtains and the light switch.
Sheep's bones
Just to the left of the totem pole at floor level of the primitive dwellings cabinet lies a section of a kitchen floor from the house at number 97 St Aldate's which was made entirely from sheep's bones.
Severed fingers
Magic cabinet in the far right corner.
The donation box
Facing you as you walk, this houses several weird carved figures which bow and whose eyes light up when you put your money in. It's a bit scary actually.

MIDDLE FLOOR
Self-torture instruments
Past cabinet 45 on the left-hand wall. Open the thickest bottom drawer, inside you'll find a grizzly collection of home torture equipment once used by the Dervishes. One particular object, a spiked ball for insertion and rotation in the eye socket might, however, put you off your dinner.
The tiniest doll in the world
(1cm long) in the games cabinet on the right wall.
Opposite this in the surgical instruments cabinet lies a small box with an alarming-looking spikey object inside and has the eye-watering label – 'for operations on the penis'

The world's tiniest doll, said to have once been owned by Ronnie Corbett

in its eyes. Look out also for the Sussex witch trapped in a bottle, who, if ever released, is said to cause terrible revenge on the world.

I could go on forever but needless to say this museum is just terrific and anyone with a love of the bizarre and mysterious will not be disappointed. Allow a couple of hours for a good look around and if you're feeling adventurous seek out Brian or Roger, two of the curators who could take you on a Zulu trail or show you some of the lesser known exhibits tucked away in the dark corners of the museum. And of course they're both as suitably eccentric as you'd expect from anyone working here.

Pitt Rivers Annex
60 Banbury Road (01865) 274726
Open 1pm-4.30pm Mon-Sat

While the archaeology section is nothing to get into raptures about, in keeping with the nature of the Pitt Rivers it has a suitably bizarre but beautiful collection of musical instruments ranging from Javanese Gamelans and nose flutes to toy telephones, a squeaky frog and an English kettle.

Compared to its big brother, the collection here is slight but it does have a small garden round the back with a music theme where you can see a variety of plants, ranging from campanula to bamboo, used for making musical instruments.

The best bit about the place has to be that on Wednesdays the Oxford Gamelan society meet at 6pm and bash out a few tunes on this elegant instrument. If you want to come and have a listen or maybe even join them contact (01865) 723645.

Hollywell Cemetery
St Cross Road

Probably the most magical cemetery in the world. This enchanted garden of tumble-down graves and overgrown wildlife has been deliberately left this way to keep it a secure home to badgers, foxes, toads and birds who have been given consideration over the lawnmower and rake. The deeper one ventures into this graveyard, the wilder and more mysterious it becomes, as if out of some classic children's fairy story, so it's no surprise that the author of Wind in the Willows, Kenneth Grahame should be buried here*. If you're in the area it is well worth taking a leisurely wander around here, especially at dusk, when you will not be too surprised to see elves, pixies and wombles frolicking together in the undergrowth.

*more surprisingly perhaps is the grave of maverick drama critic Ken Tynan who will always be remembered as the first person to say 'fuck' on television in the 1960s, causing untold complaints and widespread panic among the middle classes

The Shark House
New High Street Headington

This incredible work of art achieved international fame in 1986 when local prankster Bill Heine became a first-time home-owner and asked his friend and sculptor John Buckley
'what can we do with this house?'

John's response was to build and install a fibre-glass shark crashing into the roof of Bill's new house.

The day Bill decided to install it, rather unsurprisingly, the police turned up to find out what he was doing
'just sticking a shark in my roof,' was the reply.

The police thought about it for a while and then conceded that there was no law against sticking a shark in your roof and left.

Bill woke the next day to find heavy rain swamping his kitchen, an army of council officials standing outside his house ready to give him a Chinese burn, and Terry Wogan on the phone. It seemed he'd made the news.

In fact, the shark house was quickly recognised all over the world as a unique piece of art, and it was this that

partly saved its skin. Bill had to fight a six-year battle with planners, councillors and other officials over its survival owing to the fact that he hadn't actually applied for planning permission. The council at least realised that it was something worth keeping but couldn't handle the idea of it sticking out of Bill's roof, and at one time suggested putting the shark in a local swimming pool, which as you can imagine, kind of misses the point.

In the meantime, it was attracting more supporters than critics and even had scouts camping on it for 21 hours in 1988. Resident shark supporter and unofficial archivist June Whitehouse once famously said: *'It doesn't smell, it doesn't make a noise and it's not illegally parked, so what's the problem?'*

But the battle continued until finally it was left in the hands of the (then) secretary of State Michael Hesseltine, who, legend has it, came to Oxford, walked up and down the street several times, and finally declared in a fit of rare clarity – *There has to be a place for the strange and downright quirky in our planning regulations.'*

And so finally the shark was safe.

One resident couldn't afford the real thing...

HOW TO HAVE A CHEESY DAY IN OXFORD

If you've already succumbed to buying yourself a novelty Oxford teddy bear, University sweat-shirt and had your photo taken outside the Sheldonian then you might as well go the whole hog.

Bus Tour

Every 15 minutes (01865) 240105
£7 concessions available
Stops include Oxford Station, Pembroke College on St Aldates, Sheldonian Theatre on Broad Street and Gloucester Green bus station

Join the happy throngs of tourists as they barge and elbow their way to the top for a front seat leaving you sat at the back with a stroppy German teenager with halitosis. For the rather steep fare of £7 you can have someone pointing out the sights of Oxford which, if you bothered to get off your lazy backside, you could walk around and see for free.

The bus tours can be organised through the Tourist Information or you can just go find one of their stops and wait for one to turn up.

The Oxford Story

6 Broad Street (01865)790055 open 9.30am-5pm every day Adults £4.50, concs £3.50

Belittled by locals and sneered at by students, this is however one of the most entertaining experiences you can have in Oxford if you love tacky tourist trips, or have taken enough medication beforehand. Your journey starts with handing over your well-earned cash to a few weary individuals looking particularly uncomfortable in period costume. From here you will be transported into a 'realistic' common room for a short film which provides a truly forgettable glimpse of how students play croquet and wear corduroy jackets in seminars. The pleasant classical music does, however, allow you a moment to remove yourself from the video and think about what you'll eat tonight and if Eastenders will see yet another character die in a tragic scaffolding accident.

Before arriving at one of the world's scariest indoor roller coasters, carefully study the student's room and then ask yourself how many students actually have, not one, but, three Barclays Bank posters on the wall? Hmm, couldn't be a spot of subtle advertising, could it?? Whatever happened to Che Guevara, Trainspotting and that girl on the tennis court scratching her bum?

And so, to the moment of truth. Are you brave enough to ride Oxford's equivalent of the corkscrew? For this achingly slow ghost-train-style ride you sit behind a desk (nice touch) accompanied, by way of headphones, with your host for the journey Timmy Mallett or Magnus Magnusson. If you're doing this for the cheese factor then Mr Mallet is your natural choice, although surprisingly he isn't that irritating (he must have had a lobotomy). What is irritating though, is that if you're taller than 5 foot 11 inches (my height) the headphone leads are just that little bit too short, so when Timmy asks you to turn your head to the right to see a waxwork model of Isaac Newton you end up half strangled.

On your roller-coaster journey you'll find out about lots of people who discovered stuff, kings who wore platform shoes and how to make a baked Alaska. If you look carefully enough you'll even spot the Buddha. What's he doing here???

At the end you can peruse the gift shop which excels in useless tat. Best viewed in mid-winter when you won't be surrounded by gangs of marauding foreign students.

Museum of Oxford
Tues-Fri 10am-4pm, Sat 10am-5pm, Sun12am-4pm £2/1.50

The kind of place I remember from school trips, with faded cardboard cut-outs of Roman soldiers and plastic models of medieval villages. Nothing to get excited about I'm afraid, kind of a walk-around version of the Oxford Story with more of a slant towards socio-political history rather than academic history. Highlights include a skeleton, a mammoth's tooth and a collection of marmalade jars. I'll spare you the lowlights.

A SPOTTERS GUIDE
TO OXFORD CELEBRITIES

What better way to spend your afternoon than going all gooey-eyed and weak-kneed at having stumbled across your favourite celebrity? Oxford is home to a motley collection of comedians, musicians and authors, all of whom will be more than delighted to spend their free time autographing your breasts and listening to you repeat their catchphrases. I wish you every success with your sleuthing.

ROWAN ATKINSON

The rubbery-faced comedian can be occasionally found in Gee's restaurant. He doesn't revel in adoration, so if you do see him, try and snigger at a discrete distance.

Worth 30 points

DR GRAHAME GARDEN

The former Goodie can be spotted most mornings at the train station having a fag or two, waiting to pop into London for his millionth appearance on 'I'm Sorry I haven't a Clue.' If you see him, pinch his fags until he reveals to you the rules for Mornington Crescent.

Worth 15 points

RICHARD BRANSON

The self-made millionaire and publicist lives just outside Oxford in Kidlington but often balloons into Cornmarket trying to blag free CDs from his former empire. Notorious for borrowing taxi money and never re·paying it, if you see him walking towards you looking confused and patting his pockets, run away.

Worth 20 points

MICKEY FROM SUPERGRASS

Mickey from Supergrass
The band's bassist and occasional vocalist can be spotted in Mothercare buying nappies for the wee ones at home. If spotted, tell him he's great.

Worth 15 points

THOM YORKE (SINGER OF RADIOHEAD)

Thom can be found loitering around the mushroom section of the big Tesco's at the Cowley roundabout. Whether he's seeking solace in the world of edible fungi or in need of inspiration for a new song, only the great man knows himself. If you do spot him try and avoid fawning or asking to make babies with him as he has a reputation for being shy and aloof.

If you really want to impress him keep a couple of flyagarics in your pocket and if you're lucky enough to spot him, thrust them in his hand, bow slightly, then walk away.

Worth 25 points

COLIN DEXTER

I've no idea what he looks like (except he describes himself as short and bald) and I'm sure you haven't either but the writer of Inspector Morse is legendary in these parts for taking every opportunity to draw attention to himself and has even been known to sport a T-shirt with the motto 'Dexter Here' on it. Also known to talk to himself on buses. If spotted, approach with caution.

Worth 10 points

MARK GARDNER (EX SINGER OF RIDE)

The one-time God of floppy hair and shoe-gazing can be seen around the Cowley Road pubs and venues. If you see him tell him you're forming a Ride tribute band and get him to demonstrate that fey lop-sided look.
Worth 10 points

JEREMY PAXMAN

I don't know for sure that he lives here but he's seen a lot wandering around Broad Street practicing being rude to students for University Challenge. If you see him tell him his head is shaped like a horse's then run away before he can think of a sarcastic reply.
Worth 25 points

If you've been missed out of our spotter's guide and feel that you ought to be included, please write to us finishing the following sentence.

I think I'm famous enough to be in your guide because

....

Please enclose £10 and a signed photo. If you have appeared on Channel 6 or have just been an extra in Inspector Morse, this will not be sufficient.

A SPOTTERS GUIDE TO LOCAL ECCENTRICS

BILL HEINE (THE SHARK MAN)

Raconteur, prankster, spokesman for the needy, egomaniac and moustachioed monster, Bill Heine has been described as all of these and more by the people of Oxford. One of the town's more controversial and colourful local celebrities, Bill is best known for being the owner of the Shark house and getting up the noses of local councillors and politicians. Unmissable with his white bouffant locks and dashing moustache, you'll find Bill involved in charity events, endlessly campaigning for equal rights for others, and still finding time to run his own local radio chat show and front his own TV program on Channel 6. Look for him out and about with his camera crew making citizen's arrests on crack dealers and baby snatchers, and against all odds keeping his hair immaculate and managing to find time to wave at his admiring public.

What the locals think of him:

'The old ladies love him, he's a local Anne Robinson.'
'I don't like his Hollywood tan.'
'A generous man who always throws good parties.'
'Who?'
Worth 10 points

Mac

Often described as 'bald and scary', Mac is a long-time music promoter, notorious boozer and singer in one of Oxford's longest-running bands – Arthur Turner's Lovechild.

This is the man with more stories to tell about your favourite rock stars than Jonathan King. If you meet him, be armed with a bottle of whiskey and don't expect to leave his clutches until it's empty. You might have a hangover from hell the next day but you'll probably also have some great tales to tell the grandchildren.

Worth 10 points, 25 if sober

Justin Time (Oxford's Official Jester)

Taught to juggle by Timmy Mallett, through the power of television, Justin quickly developed his magic powers to become what he is today – the official jester of Oxford. His inauguration on January 13th, 2000 saw Justin taking an oath to *'bring merriment and happiness to the people of Oxford'* and he can often be seen around town entertaining people with his juggling, stilt-walking and magic tricks. His notoriety and fame has spread so much these days, that he once cancelled a kids' party at Blackbird Leys when he had an emergency royal summons to go to Prince Charles 50th birthday bash. After turning up dressed in full jester gear the Queen looked him up and down and said-

'So what are you here for??'

Found down the Cowley Road, Magic Café or just about any pub you care to think of.

Worth 15 points, 30 if wearing a tie

Colonel Mustard

The Colonel, also known as Captain Tap, is probably Oxford's eldest known busker (there is a record of him in the Doomsday book), and can be spotted most weekends, somewhere around Carfax and Cornmarket, wearing some wild regalia and tap-dancing. This grizzly old legend, invariably dressed in an improbable hat or coat, came second place in the 1981 Bognor Regis Opportunity Knocks competition, so give him the respect he's due. Worth 20 points

Cowley Road posse

The Scottish Street Cleaner in full regalia, the guy with the bone through his nose and the Reverend in his dog collar propping up a bar or two are just a few of the fruitier characters you're likely to spot on a typical day's wander up the Cowley Road. Each worth 5 points

---

If you've been missed out of our eccentrics guide and feel that you ought to be included, please write to us finishing the following sentence.

I think I'm odd enough to be in your eccentrics guide because...fish fingers...............

....

Yes I'm over 18, live near the Cowley Road, and dress in an alarming fashion. ☐

An Introduction to
Oxford
University

There are 39 colleges dotted around Oxford, each existing as a separate entity and ranging from 50 to over 600 years old. Some are tiny and can be easily missed, like Mansfield College located in the basement of Marks and Spencers, while others, like Christ Church and Magdalen, are majestic in size, containing parks and huge gardens within their grounds.

With the exception of some of the very modern buildings, the ubiquitous design for every college is the quad, which, taken from the tradition of monastries, meant the college buildings would always be inward-looking, a spiritual metaphor from the days when Christianity and religious training were the very focal point of college life.

In the last 20 years, the University has been making an effort to re-address the balance of men and women, and with the last all-male college disappearing 16 years ago, the number of female students has been ever-growing. Equally the balance of public school and state school students is getting better; prejudice is in decline and only 12 months ago the first student from Scunthorpe was admitted into the University.

Most colleges are free to visit but opening times vary wildly, some are open all day every day, others for just five minutes on Shrove Tuesday. A few even charge steep entrance fees, but as long as you don't walk around in a Hawaiian shirt taking photographs you should slip unnoticed into the grounds.

Visitors are usually allowed to wander freely around the quads, chapel, dining hall and gardens but everywhere else is strictly out of bounds. Despite this, and the 'NO ENTRY' signs, every year I hear stories of tourists in search of toilets inadvertently bursting into a student's bedroom to find, not the urinals, but a pasty-faced youth in his underpants hunched over a copy of Ovid.

Without much background information on the colleges, when you've been in one or two they may all start to look suspiciously similar. After much consideration therefore, we have focused heavily on our ten favourite colleges with maps, places of interest and juicy stories to get the best out of each. The other 29, incidentally, all resemble Oriel except St Anne's which looks like Sainsburys and St Peter's which often gets mistaken for Manpower.

An A-Z of University
Traditions
&Terminology

Balls

Once the exams are over in June, the parties really begin and all over the colleges lavish balls are held, the biggest, which is known as the Commemorative Ball, being at either Magdalen, Worcester or New College. Ticket prices for these average around £100 each so it's not surprising that there are clubs such as the Oxford Stunt factory whose sole mission is to gate-crash as many balls as possible. Expect string ensembles, bouncy castles, free booze, fairground rides, gambling and if a band are playing, chances are it'll be Bad Manners.

If you want to try gate-crashing, stick on some overalls and stride purposefully into the college carrying a bucket of water. It works about five times out of every ten although if this book sells well, your odds might go down somewhat...

Beating the Bounds

If you happened to be shopping in Marks and Spencer's on Ascension day you may be alarmed to see twenty or so men and women enter, proceed to beat a metal cross in the floor with willow sticks and then leave again. This spectacle, however bizarre it may seem, would have been fairly  common to witness centuries ago. Parish authorities then had a civil duty to look after their own people and in order to assert where their parish boundaries were, they would walk along them one day each year and beat them with sticks. Typically, Oxford decided to uphold the tradition and so every Ascension Day, in the morning, the parishes of St Mary the Virgin (SMV) and St Michael of North Gate (SMNG) go around the town giving the walls a good walloping. It seems that M&S built over one of the boundaries and they are obliged once a year to let the loonies in. Look out for the glass case half way down the store on the left hand side bearing the original boundary stone.

Bulldogs

These guys are the last vestiges from when Oxford University had its own Police Force to keep student discipline in order. They can still be seen outside Christ Church college in their bowler hats. Why only Christ Church chose to keep them I don't know, maybe they have the naughtiest students.

Bumping

You'll probably notice as you wander around the colleges, that in the Quads will be written stuff like Merton bumped Balliol, Christ Church bumped Magdalen or possibly Roger bumped Charlotte.

This refers to the rowing races known as Torpids and Eights. In these two inter-college races the boats are lined up equal distance from each other tip to tail in lines of ten. Then they set off down the river. If a boat in 9th position catches up with the one in front and bumps it, they will swap places. There are four races, and if a team bump the team in front on all four occasions putting them into position number one, then they are Head of The River and win a Teasmaid.

Collections

This is the name given to all the examinations that the students sit at the beginning of every term, although rather confusingly the end of term report, where a student is congratulated by their tutor or told to pull their socks up, is also known as a collection.

Dining Societies

Most colleges have exclusive dining societies to which students may be invited to join if their pedigree is up to it. Particularly popular in the 30s, there was often a debauched and sinister element to them. One Brasenose society with 12 members, was notorious for laying 13 spaces to dinner, the extra one being of course for the devil. Nowadays however it's more twits in tails and white ties trashing a place then giving the owner a cheque with lots of 0s at the end of it.

Oronyatekka Dining Society

The origins of this society stem from the last century when the Prince of Wales was invited to Canada to hunt with some of its native Indians. As a consequence, one chief's son was invited to study at Teddy college where he distressed the Principal by eloping with his daughter. The story has a happy ending though, as years later he returned after inheriting a fortune and donated lots of money to his old college. His portrait now hangs there and is rather dubiously celebrated by this dining society.

The group meet once a year for dinner dressed up as Indians and proceed to talk pretend 'Indian' all night (matchbox would be white man magic box make fire, etc). Then they are reputed to rampage through town making whooping noises and ending up at Park End sat in a circle around a pretend fire and smooching to Paul McCartney's Pipes of Peace.

Essay

'A collection of other people's thoughts disguised to look like your own, in the judging of which originality is heavily penalised.'

Graham Chapman A Liar's Autobiography

Exams

In the middle of June, don't be surprised to see students wearing pink, white or red carnations; this will tell you they're in exams. They wear white for their first exam, pink for the middle and red for their last. Keep an eye out especially for those with red carnations. Tradition decrees that after their last exam has finished, friends and strangers alike will be at liberty to pelt them with eggs and flour and empty tins of baked beans over their heads as a way of saying well done. The pelting takes places over several days, culminating in the High Street near the examination hall, although any student caught in the vicinity of the examination hall with so much as a champagne bottle is liable to find themselves caught and fined by the University.

Feuds

There are many long-standing feuds between a number of colleges, none seeming more intense than that of Balliol and Trinity. Legend has it that at one time Balliol was down on its luck, with poor finances and in a bad state of repair. So as a way of rubbing salt into their wounds, the Dean of Trinity took great delight in wandering round Balliol during the night, throwing stones through any windows that remained unbroken. The feud continues to this day and the emergence of the Harry Lime society in Balliol seems to secure its future. Their sole aim is to apply lime coloured paint to any sacred cows of Trinity College, the most famous being the time they painted Trinity's boat house lime green one year. Another story tells of how they killed the coy carp in Trinity's fountain after turning the water lime green with a dye. It wasn't the dye that killed the fish but the washing up liquid they thoughtfully added afterwards to give it that foamy effect.

GCR and MCR (Graduate common room and Middle common room)
The hang-out in every college for fellows, post-grads and dons where they can visit the tuck shop, play conkers and have a crafty ciggie.

JCR (Junior common room)
Lounge area for all undergraduates, like a 6th form common room, but in most cases, less appealing, especially when full of students.

Lodgings and Dinner

All undergraduates lodge in the college grounds in their first year but most have to seek accommodation outside the college after this. Food is provided for all students in the college and formal wear is often required for the second sitting except at St Catherine's where rollneck and flares are permitted.

Lingo
Talking to the students for the first time can be intimidating and even a little frightening, owing to the vast array of bizarre and alarming languages exclusive to each college. If, however, you can befriend or tame one of them for just a few days they might take you into their confidence and teach you to say something like –

'Cynthia was using her face on this awful mirkin at the ball yesterday and within five minutes was giving him a real good jeffing.'

Jeffing – from the verb 'to Jeff', meaning to snog in a cinematic or nauseating way.

Using her face – to become animated and charming

Mirkin – any student who isn't from Oriel but whose knuckles still drag along the ground when he walks.

Matriculation and Graduation
See the students buffed up and manicured at the Sheldonian Theatre. Matriculation is the formal entry of every student into Oxford while Graduation is the final farewell. Seeing as though Graduation takes place in the same building and in a similar fashion, it would be hard to tell the difference between the two at a glance, apart from the fact that students are only allowed to wear their mortar boards after graduation while all matriculation students have to carry theirs.

During graduation the whole of Broad Street is filled with brimming parents and camera flashes. If you see a miserable looking bunch with strange haircuts, don't worry, it's just the art students realising that a future teaching or working at Macdonald's awaits them.

MA's

Unlike every other university in the UK where you have to study hard for another year to achieve this qualification, in Oxford all a graduate needs to obtain one of these is a crisp ten-pound note.

Oxford Time

If you hear Christ Church bell ringing at 9.05pm when your watch says 9pm that's because some students' clocks still run on Oxford time. The city is 1 degree 15 minutes west of the Greenwich Mean Time which means bugger all to me but it purports to be the reason why.

Punks

According to a law passed in the 1970s, every college must have at least one Punk or Goth to add to its credibility (even though they're usually just public school boys with an identity crisis). If you visit the colleges during term-time keep a look out for them, they love having their pictures taken with tourists.

Rustication

Any student proving to make enough of a nuisance of himself might find him or herself in this predicament, which means they are packed off home for the year as punishment for a terrible crime, the ultimate being to have copied someone else's essay. Oscar Wilde fell victim after returning to Magdalen two weeks late into term following a holiday in Greece. Despite this he still got a first.

Sconcing

This is an old tradition often practised at formal dinners and drinking societies whereby if a student (or don for that matter) challenges another to drink a yard of ale (2 and a half pints) they must accept the challenge. But it seems that Christ Church students can claim immunity to the challenge on the grounds of being 'housemen' ie belonging to the house of Christ. This of course hasn't helped dispel the myth by Pembroke students that they're nothing more than a bunch of lily-livered shandy drinkers.

Scouts

A job done almost exclusively by women, these are the cleaners who sort out the rooms in colleges for the students. In the past, their unofficial role was as the confidant of the student, and often a surrogate mother/son relationship would foster. In Edwardian times wealthy students would often leave the contents of their wardrobe to their scout, who in those days would have been male. These links have loosened over time and all a student is likely to leave now is a copy of Razzle and a couple of odd socks.

In Cambridge, scouts are known as 'Bedders', which suggests that the unofficial mother/son role may have extended towards an unhealthy Oedipus complex.

Single Sex Colleges

There are no more exclusively all-male colleges in Oxford, although St Hilda's by Magdalen Bridge is the last to remain exclusive to women and the young ladies there are known affectionately as Hildabeasts.

Students and Dons

A Don is anyone who takes tutorials or lectures in the colleges and a student is to whom they give the tutorial, except in Christ Church where the Dons are rather confusingly known as Students and the students are referred to as Rimmers. Hence the phrase *'I can't come out tonight I've got to do a spot of rimming with my room-mate.'*

Visitor

A visitor to a college doesn't mean a tourist but rather confusingly means someone who is a patron of the college eg. The Queen is a Visitor of Christ Church and Fidel Castro is a Visitor of Wadham.

Zebra

There are no zebras in Oxford.

Christ Church

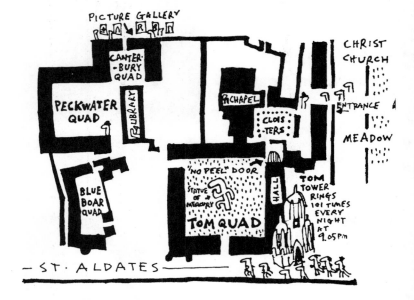

Christ Church (also known as The House)

St Aldate's (01865) 276140 open 9am-5pm Mon-Sun £3 admission, gallery £1

The largest and most visited of all Oxford's colleges, Christ Church is rich, has a diverse student population and over the years has produced a wealth of prominent politicians, writers and thinkers. So it's not suprising then that its fame and majestic appearance mean that it is sometimes mistaken as the only college in Oxford by dozy tourists.

In the middle of the college lies the magnificent Tom Quad, the largest quadrangle in Oxford. In the centre, the God Mercury does his best Bruce Forsyth impression whilst all around are the rooms and quarters of many important historical figures as well as the odd loony.

In the far right-hand corner of the Quad under the stairs of the Great Hall, lies a door, with the graffiti 'No Peel' burned into it. This dates back to the mid-17th Century when the Black Death was scouring the land and the college doctor (in the latter stages of Syphilis and as mad as a brush) prescribed raw potato peelings as preventative medicine for the plague. The Christ Church students were forced to eat whole plates of the stuff with their breakfast and evening meals to keep away the dreaded disease. The graffiti appeared after a month of protests from the students and this revolting diet was quietly dropped when the good Doctor was found wandering around Peckwater Quad 'hurling lemons and other citrus fruit at the students, and showing his gentalia to anyone who approached him.'

Up the stairs, you'll find the Grand Dining Hall littered with majestic paintings of Christ Church men and a few kings and queens, while a portrait of Charles Dodgeson (Lewis Carroll) hangs on your immediate right when you go in. Dinner is served twice in the evening, once at 6.30pm and then again at 7.20pm where only formal wear is allowed. To enter the hall for second dinner, according to college rules, jacket and tie must be worn at all times. Because of the ambiguity however, of what to wear 'downstairs', shorts, underpants and ladies knickers have all been worn at some time by cheeky students.

Christ Church Picture Gallery
At the Merton Street entrance at the back of Christ Church by Canterbury quad is a small basement gallery with a modest collection for anyone passionate about Renaissance art or sketches from old masters. If you're visiting with children get them to look out for the gory Strozzi painting of Judith from the Old Testament story, holding the severed head of Holofernes. A hastily improvised story comparing Holofernes to Kenny from South Park should keep them interested for a good 15 seconds.

Christ Church Chapel
I have heard that a way to avoid Christ Church's steep admission fee is to claim you are going to the chapel to pray. Although I haven't tried it, there does seem to be a ring of truth in this, as the chapel is the official Cathedral for the diocese of Oxfordshire, so look pious, fake the local accent and you'll get in.

In the 1980s this tiny cathedral came upon a unique way of getting some much-needed funds for repairs to its roof. It had installed a jukebox of 'holy hits' ranging from 'Jerusalem' to 'Spirit in the Sky', which you could play for 50p a go. But complaints arose when a copy of Too Drunk to Fuck by the Dead Kennedy's was sneaked in by some wily students and the embarrassed Dean had the jukebox removed.

Heroes and Villains

John Locke (Philosopher)
Charles Dodgeson (aka
author Lewis Carroll)
WH Auden (Poet)

Tom Tower

Up on the top left of Christ Church, overlooking the Head of the River, is this famous tower built by Sir Christopher Wren. Hanging in here is the seven-ton mass of Great Tom, a bell which still chimes 101 times at five past nine every night. This was the old curfew bell, rung once for the 101 students of Christ Church to remind them to be back in college grounds. Nowadays it is used by the students as a reminder that Happy Hour in The Bear is just about to end.

William Buckland

One of Christ Church's most notorious eccentrics was William Buckland who, in the 1900s, was first professor of Geology here and lodged in one corner of Tom Quad.

Buckland, not content with keeping a bizarre ménagerie of livestock in his room, (which included a jackal and a bear), was also quite

WILLIAM BUCKLAND EATS HEART OF LOUIS XIV

exotic in his palatal tastes too and rather enjoyed eating them. His dinner guests would often be bemused, and a little horrified, when presented with mice fried in batter, stewed badger and even worm fritters. In fact, as his eccentricity grew, he rather fancied attempting to eat every living thing. Legend has it that whilst dining with the owners of Nuneham Park one evening, he was proudly shown a shrivelled piece of flesh, and asked to guess what it was. Before he could be stopped, Buckland had gobbled it up. His hosts were mortified, he had just swallowed their most treasured heir loom – the heart of King Louis 14th .

All Souls College

All Souls College

High Street (01865) 279379 Open 2pm-4pm Mon-Fri free admission

Set up in the 15th century as a place of prayer and learning for the secular clergy, this college takes its name from 'all souls of the faithfully departed', a remembrance of the dead from the Hundred Years War with France in the 14th and 15th century. Nowadays it is a mysteriously quiet graduate college for the élite. You don't apply to get in here, you get elected, although the most outstanding undergraduates can come and sit some gruelling exams to try and gain entrance.

There isn't a great deal to see compared to many other colleges but because it is such an enigmatic place, curiosity should get the better of you. Its most famous architectural features are the twin gothic towers in the Great Quad overlooking Catte Street and the large sundial, built by Christopher Wren, which sits on the wall of the Codrington library.

Its chapel was said to be a regular haunt of Yeats who, although he never studied at All Souls, would hang out there and write poems on magic.

Midnight has come and the great Christ Church bell
And many a lesser bell sound through the room;
And it is all Soul's night
And two long glasses brimmed with muscatel
Bubble upon the table. A ghost may come;
For it is a ghost's right
His element is so fine
Being sharpened by his death
To drink from the wine-breath
While our gross palates drink from the whole wine.
From All Soul's Night by WB Yeats

ALL SOULS OR BUST!

A game for one lonely player who has to use his intellect, table manners and nepotism to get into this prestigious college. The rules of which are based on spurious rumours and idle gossip.

Round one

You have three hours to write as much as you can on one word. The word could be anything from Politics to Beekeeping depending how cruel they're feeling that day. This is followed by a translation paper of which the college will choose the language for you. It could be anything from Esperanto to Welsh so you better start brushing up.

Round Two

Well done, they were obviously impressed with your Welsh accent and extensive knowledge about bees. You will now be invited for an interview with some of the members of the college. This can be anyone that's ever studied here so be prepared for quite a large ensemble. First you will be asked to name the Kings and Queens of England in reverse order and then there'll be a rigorous grilling of your family background, who you know, and how much power your father has in Westminster. Namedrop as many important people as you can, especially anyone involved in politics or the media and above all else, try and be related to Lawrence of Arabia.

Round three

Good going, you're nearly there. You will finally be invited to dine with the college members. More than any other time in your life be totally on your guard. To discover your true pedigree and etiquette you will most likely be served boiled artichokes and spaghetti. All eyes will be on you at all times so try and avoid slurping sounds and at all costs don't suck the spaghetti from the plate. Whilst dining your peers will deliberately try and trick you by passing the port the wrong way and giving you the wrong spoon with which to eat your soup. Remember to be vigilant at all times and under no circumstances get drunk and start telling mother-in-law jokes.

CONGRATULATIONS YOU MADE IT!!

You are now a fellow of All Souls college and as such may stay here
for up to seven years with free meals, lodgings and a salary.
And don't worry, academic work here is not compulsory, you can
sit around in your pants all day and watch Richard and Judy if you want.
Welcome to heaven.

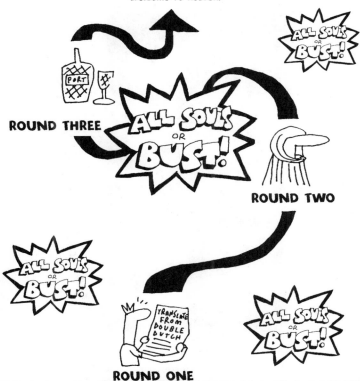

ROUND THREE

ALL SOULS
or
BUST!

ROUND TWO

ROUND ONE

Oxford's oddest tradition – The Mallard Feast

At the beginning of every new century, tradition decrees that after dinner on All Souls Day, Fellows and Masters grab sticks and torches and go wandering around the college grounds and roof-tops pretending to search for the ghost of a mallard duck. Lord Mallard, who carries a long stick and wears a plastic beak around his mouth, heads the search, then, after giving up the ghost, everybody celebrates and sings the Mallard Song (the lyrics of which seem to be a closely guarded secret of the college).

The reason for this daft tradition seems to stem from the fact that when the college foundations were being laid, a mallard was found in one of the ditches. It still begs the question 'why?' and also 'why don't they all go looking for earthworms, millipedes and moles as well?', but who's to argue with such a wonderfully ludicrous tradition?

The next Mallard Feast is expected to take place on All Souls day (January 14th) 2001. Be there or be square.

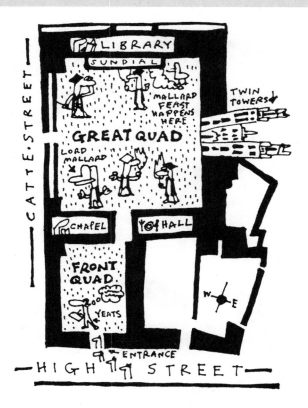

Oriel College

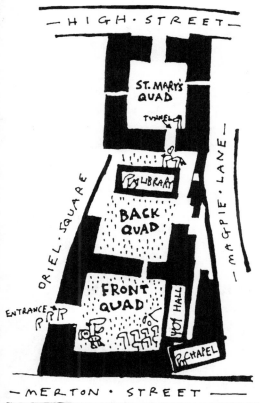

Oriel College
Oriel Square (01865) 276555
open 2pm-5pm Mon-Sun
free admission

For many centuries this college's official name was – 'The house of the blessed Mary in the Oxford, commonly called Oriel, of the foundation of King Edward the Second of famous memory, sometime King of England.' then one day someone suggested just calling it 'Oriel', and everyone was relieved.

Originally a training ground for prominent priests, in the 19th century Oriel became a powerhouse of intellectuals, but since the war its reputation has been principally for rowing, drama and music. One of its most celebrated students was intrepid explorer Sir Walter Raleigh who brought back a pound of potatoes and Twenty Marlboros from his travels, which proved popular with the masses. Every summer the Front Quad plays host to a Shakespearean production, which is a perfect way of experiencing this college.

The tunnel that leads from Middle Quad to Back Quad was once the scene of a minor scandal during the First World War. The girls from

Somerville College had been housed in the Back Quad while their college was taken over by the medical services during the First World War and to stop the men in Oriel getting too aquainted with the girls, the tunnel was bricked up. Mysteriously, however, a hole appeared and legend has it that a few cherries were popped that night. Not taking any more chances, the Provost of Oriel and the Principle of Somerville went down to guard the tunnel and remained there day and night for the rest of the war to uphold the dignity of the colleges.

Dastardly deeds

For many years, Oriel was proud of its unbroken record of being Head of the River but in the winter of 1991, the Secretary of the University Boat Club is said to have put up a notice in secret in Exeter College forbidding all rowing practice on the river owing to the danger of ice. Oriel of course never saw the message and so set out the next morning for their usual practice. After 15 minutes they too decided it was dangerous to row but that was enough time for them to get nobbled by the boat club for breaking the rules.

At the hearing The Secretary is reported to have clapped his hands in glee and said *'let's dick Oriel'* and they were penalised for boating illegally and dropped four places from Head of the river where they had been for 20 years.

I am not a tortoise I am a human being

Like many other colleges Oriel used to have a tortoise as a mascot. During the inter-war period, however, the students thought it was getting lonely so they bought it a female to keep it company and some months later a baby tortoise appeared, which they christened George Whalley after a Fellow. The students as a joke sent a telegram to the Times which read – To Testudo* of Oriel college, a son George Whalley. *The Times, unable to take a joke, was horrified to discover what it had printed and to add insult to injury the students later admitted that George had actually been purchased from Oxford market anyway…*

*latin for tortoise

A cheeky tale

Many years ago I came here to see a production of Hamlet. It had been raining heavily for two days and we, the audience, were seated on a raised platform underneath a canopy of overlapping sheets of transparent tarpaulin. It wasn't raining that afternoon but there was a cold wind whipping around us as we huddled together watching the play.

Hamlet, alone on the stage, was contemplating life and death in his famous soliloquy when, unexpectedly, the wind whipped up one of the sheets of tarpaulin from above our heads, suddenly freeing about 10 gallons of rainwater that had been trapped there. In a short but torrential downpour, it managed to completely drench one poor sod who was sat underneath.

If that wasn't enough entertainment, watching Hamlet giggle his way through 'to be or not to be' made it indeed a moment of rare comedy I shall never forget. Thank you Oriel and Aeolus, God of Wind.

Not the most progressive of colleges, Oriel was the last college to admit female undergraduates into its folds and today in the college bar women will only be served half pints in ladies glasses and are still required to wear ankle-length skirts.

Corpus Christi

Corpus Christi

Merton Street (01865) 276700 open 1.30pm-4.30pm Mon-Sun free admission

With a reputation for liberalism and friendliness, Corpus Christi, though sandwiched between Merton and Christ Church, should not be overlooked, as it is one of the smallest but most beautiful colleges in Oxford. Founded in 1517 by Richard Fox, legend has it that he was blind when the college was completed so, to avoid his disappointment, he was led around the front quad twenty three times to make it seem bigger than it was.

Corpus Christi's best-loved feature is its sundial in the centre of Front Quad, by which one can calculate the time not only by the sun but also the moon, although being set to Oxford time, it's always five minutes fast. At the top of the sundial sits a majestic golden pelican which was part of the coat of arms of its founder and is the most common symbol associated with the college today. In fact animals seem to crop up a lot in Corpus Christi's history. In the Middle Ages a fox, three owls and several bees were kept chained up as college mascots and for many years now Corpus Christi has been involved in the rather bizarre annual tortoise race between Balliol and Brasenose. There is even an official role of 'Custodian of the Tortoise' in the JCR. The current tortoise is

Hermione, although she doesn't actually belong to the college but is loaned by one of the professors.

A few years ago there was a small scandal when Corpus Christi was discovered to have given their tortoise a line of speed before the race to make it go faster. Despite this it didn't win, but just stood around shaking and grinding its gums for a few hours.

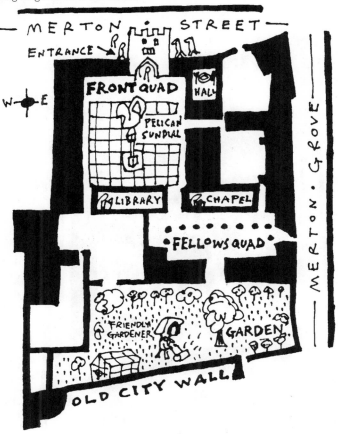

There are 117 gargoyles around Corpus Christi so you probably won't spot them all but do look out for the carving of the bird feeding its young in the corner of College Tower. Pass through Front Quad and the tiny cloisters until you get to the garden at the back and here you will be rewarded with a great view of Fellows garden, Christ Church gardens and the meadows. Finally look out for David the gardener, if he's not too busy and likes the look of you, he'll probably share a few good tales about the place.

Merton College

Merton College

Merton Street (01865) 276310 open Mon-Fri 2pm-4pm weekends 10am-4pm
Free admission, £1 for tour of the library and Max Beerbohm's room.

Located down the quiet cobbled antiquity of Merton Street away from the
bustle and pollution of The High, this college, founded in 1264, is probably the
one that most deserves the title of being Oxford's first real college.

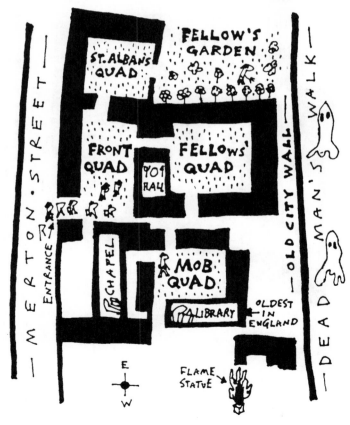

On the far right inside Merton lies Mob quad, the oldest quad in Oxford and blueprint for many of the others in Oxford and Cambridge, while at the back of the college stands part of the old city wall. A good nose around should reveal a statue in the shape of a flame. This was placed there to honour Andrew Irvine, a student who perished near the summit of Mount Everest in 1924. To this day no-one knows if he was on his way up or on his way down. If the latter, he'd would have been the first to scale that wretched mountain.

One of the best ways of experiencing a college like Merton is to visit in the summer evenings when the college puts on a series of candlelit concerts in its chapel. On occasions like this, hidden away from the modern part of the city, the visitor could easily feel transported back in time 100 years to the days when the likes of TS Elliot would have been here. Elliot didn't romanticise about the town though, Oxford wasn't much to his liking as he explained –

'As an American I have always enjoyed the company of women but in Oxford there seem to be none.'

The tour of the Old Library and Max Beerbohm's Quarters

The library, complete with all its musty smells, decomposing knowledge and silent foundations, was set up in the 14th century and is one of the oldest surviving of its age. Many of the original books are in Latin and the one still chained to the bookcase is a reminder of how precious they were in those days and could not be removed by students without a good monkey wrench.

From the library you will be taken to the room of one of Merton's most celebrated students, Max Beerbohm, who studied here in the 1890s. Max, the supposed wit of the 1890s, was famous for sending up college life in his book 'Zuleika Dobson' through the invention of the fictional St Judas College (an idea re-used in the 1980s by Tom Sharpe in his book Porterhouse Blues). Max's room has  been kept the same from that period and on the wall are some of his murals and other memorabilia from the late 19th century.

Merton's Ghosts

Being one of the oldest colleges in Oxford it would be surprising for Merton to escape the odd ghost story and in fact it boasts two.

Heroes and villains

Max Beerbohm (author of *Zuleika Dobson*)

JRR Tolkein (author of *The Hobbit, Lord of the Rings* and *Bilbo's Guide to Practical Home DIY*)

TS Elliot (author of *The Wasteland*)

One spectre, who haunts the upper library, is believed to be the ghost of Duns Scotus, a medieval philosopher and passionate academic who just couldn't bear to leave behind the world of Oxford and so vowed to remain in the library forever. Many claim to have seen his upper torso wandering through the library at midnight meaning his lower half is presumably dangling in the hallway below, yet none have as yet validated this particular theory of mine.

The other ghost is that of Colonel Francis Windebank, who was court-martialled in 1645 for having supported the King during the Civil War. He is believed to have been shot at the city wall, which now makes up the back wall of Merton College overlooking Christ Church Meadow.

His ghost is said to wander along Dead Man's Walk late at night and some say that if the cows ever moo dead on midnight, then the Colonel is taking his midnight rendezvous. Either that or the kebab van men are on the prowl again.

University College

University College
High Street (01865) 276602
Not open to the public

Opposite All Soul's and Queen's, University College is another one of these colleges hanging on to the tedious claim of being the oldest in Oxford. In fact, University was so keen to hold this title that in the 14th century a forged document appeared declaring University college to have been set up by King Alfred in the 900s. This was taken as gospel until the 19th century when at a coming out party after a lot of nervous coughing and red faces the college admitted that the documents were forged and eerrr, it wasn't really err that old and err…. twiglet anybody?

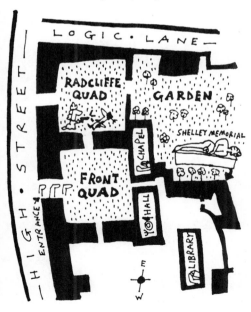

The college's two best features are its chapel, with its unusual 17th century stained-glass windows depicting stories from the Old Testament, and the Shelley Memorial. There is nothing quite like this in the whole of Oxford and for this reason it's a shame that University is permanently closed to visitors. Fear not, if you write to the domestic bursar and ask for permission to view it, he should let you in. Failing that, I leave it to your own devious minds as to how to steal a peep.

The Shelley Memorial

The English Romantic poet Percy Shelley (1792-1822), was at University for less than a year before he decided to circulate a pamphlet entitled 'The Necessity of Atheism' which caused a bit of a stink. Although he never admitted to writing it, the University got rid of him anyway for *'contumaciously refusing to answer questions about the authorship.'*

In 1891 however, his daughter-in-law had a statue of him built for the British Cemetery in Rome which proved too big to fit in the post so she offered it to University College along with a large wad of cash. University suddenly decided that perhaps Shelley wasn't all that bad and had the statue set in a separate little room inside the University.

The room features a marble slab with the naked Shelley lying on it dead, while underneath a bronze statue of the muse of poetry looks up lamenting. Over the years this room has been a gift to undergraduate japes, and Shelley's tummy banana has been painted a whole host of exotic colours while the muse has been given party hats and on one occasion the Times crossword was found sitting on its lap.

Nowadays the statue is sealed off from any potential pranksters but is definitely worth seeing in all its Victorian gaudiness.

Heroes and villains

Stephen Hawking (responsible for making black holes briefly fashionable in the late 80s, and now lecturing in Cambridge)
Armando Iannucci (comedy writer for Steve Cougan)
Richard Ingrams (founding editor of Private Eye)
Robert Boyle (Physician who developed his own law about gasses which clearly states that the volume of the pressure of gas is inversely proportional to the sum and the square of the hypotenuse)
Bill Clinton (dope-smoking sex maniac and president of the world)

Necrophelia and University College

Eminent physician Thomas Southwell rented rooms here in 1420 and became well respected for founding the College of Physicians in 1441. On a less respectable note, however, he was caught committing necrophelia with the late Duchess of Gloucester and was stuck in the Tower of London where he died the night before his execution. Since then, necrophelia has fallen out of fashion in University College and hardly any students are put to death for it these days.

The Great Shootings of 1892

In 1892 a master (with a reputation for giving the most tedious lectures in the whole of Oxford) had a daughter, who was engaged to a Fellow at the college. All seemed fine until it was discovered the man had a murky past when a wronged woman turned up at the master's lodge looking for him. She was shooed away but soon returned with a gun, hell bent on revenge. She had it in her mind to shoot the first person she saw which, unluckily for the master, happened to be him, although the wounding proved not to be fatal. The wronged woman was arrested and imprisoned, but disgrace on the Fellow led to the end of the engagement and he resigned from the college.

After the whole thing had calmed down the students did at least hope that the master's lectures were going to be a bit more interesting but all the shooting had done was to give him a pronounced stutter which made them worse than ever.

Magdalen College

Magdalen College

High Street (01865) 276000 open 2pm-dusk every day. Admission free (although there might possibly be a charge in summer)

Magdalen is one of Oxford's most impressive colleges boasting its own Deer Park, riverside walk and some beautiful architecture. Pronounce the name Mag-da-len, however, and you'll immediately reveal yourself as an impostor for the correct pronunciation is 'maudlin', although if you're an American, 'Mawwwdlin' will have to suffice.

One of the college's main architectural attractions is The Cloisters, which can be found once through the front entrance on your right through an archway. This beautiful enclosed quad is host to many strange gargoyles and statues, once brightly painted and said to have been an inspiration to CS Lewis for the stone statues in Narnia. You should be able to spot deer, camel, dragons, griffins, wrestlers, jesters and clangers along with Moses, Jacob, Goliath and several human heads.

Located behind St Swithun's Quad is Magdalen's famous Deer Park. The forty or so deer arrived in 1708 and have remained ever since, and with the exception of a few tortoises and the Wadham penguin are the only animals now kept inside college grounds.

The blue iron-gate on the far right of the college grounds will lead you to the riverside preamble which most times of the year is refreshingly peaceful. A gate and a bridge lead to an island between the branches of the Cherwell and in the middle is a water meadow also used for the deer. If you're lucky enough to be around in March and April for a few weeks the water meadow appears to be stroked by a purple mist when the fritillaries are in bloom.

On May 1st for hundreds of years Magdalen's Great Tower has played host to the choristers who at 6am sing to crowds of thousands who gather at Magdalen bridge. This probably has its roots in an old pagan tradition of celebrating fertility, although the subsequent act of students throwing themselves into the Cherwell is more likely to derive from an old Saxon tradition called the drowning of the fools.

The North Wall

After you've been around a few colleges in Oxford most start to look suspiciously similar, whereas Magdalen is a place you might happily want to spend a couple of hours in. Even its bar has a fabulous reputation, a rare thing amongst Oxford student drinking holes.

It's not surprising then that Magdalen is sometimes regarded with jealous mockery by some of the poorer colleges who can only afford a small tarmac play area for their students. In fact, there is a well-known story of one rival college, who, in the late 1890s, got so fed up with everyone marvelling at the Deer Park that it decided to outdo Magdalen once and for all by building a Giraffe Park. It was indeed a stunning sight and its fame spread quickly. Unfortunately, within a month every single one of the poor creatures had been captured by rustlers from nearby villages, and the following week a huge influx of giraffe rugs appeared at Oxford market.

Oscar Wilde

One of Oxford's most infamous undergraduates, Oscar Wilde, studied here from 1874 to 1878 where he indulged in his love of aestheticism and fresh faced young men. A brilliant scholar, Oscar is famously said to have read about his First in the Times whilst dining in The Mitre one morning.

NOTORIOUS EX-SCHOLAR. OSCAR WILDE.

Heroes and villains

Dudley Moore (pint-sized comedian and one-time partner with the late great Peter Cook)
C.S. Lewis (author of the Narnia books)
William Hague (comedian)
John Betjeman (poet)

One of the lesser-known stories about Wilde tells of how one day four students, singularly unimpressed with Wilde's foppish behaviour, decided to smash up his room. Upon finding them, Wilde, being a big fellow at well over six foot, single-handedly ejected them all and escorted the ringleader to his own room, where Wilde rolled him up in a carpet and piled furniture on top of him. He then calmly opened up this student's most expensive bottle of wine and invited any onlookers to join him in a glass.

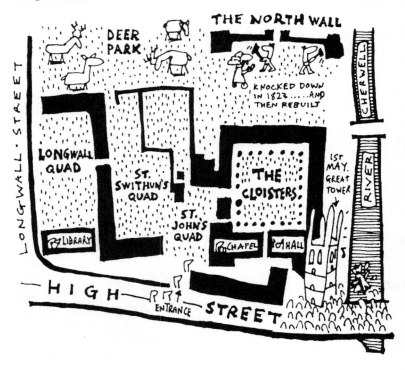

The President, The Wall, His wife, Her Moustache

At the back of the college grounds sits a rather idiosyncratic building known as the North Wall. This was the beginning of a Georgian classical quad built in the late 1700s to replace the Cloisters which were believed to be getting a bit tatty and small. The North Wall was the first part of this new wing to be built but then money ran out and so it remained. Throughout the 1800s top architects gave their ideas on what to do with it but nothing happened and there it sat.

Now it just so happened that in 1823 Magdalen had itself a rather eccentric president by the name of Martin Routh. Routh became president in 1791, and continued in this role until he died in 1854 at a ripe old age. He was known for wearing a long cassock under which his invisible feet would take tiny delicate steps giving the impression that he was on wheels. Though he kept his marbles until the end, he was a man who despised change, and continued wearing knee breeches and a wig all through the 19th century when the fashion had moved on somewhat. Because of his ardent resistance to change, it came as something of a shock to the college when on a whim one morning in 1823 Routh called in the builders at 4am and had the North Wall completely demolished. It very quickly caused a national outcry and to his great reluctance had to be painstakingly rebuilt, stone by stone, to its former glory where it still stands today.

Routh got more disagreeable as the years dragged by although he did succumb to cupid's arrow in his mid-sixties when he married Mrs Routh whose moustache was said to be legendary. In later years Routh's health declined and his steps got shorter and shorter until finally he ended up being carried from his lodgings to chapel in a sedan chair, the spectacle of which became quite a tourist attraction.

When he died, Charles Daubeny, a Magdalen scientist, who had always despised Routh's policies, took one of his wigs to a spring at Matlock in Derbyshire known to harden any object dropped in it owing to its special mineral content. So it was that Routh's wig became hard as stone and still hangs to this day in the old library.

Brasenose College

Brasenose College

Radcliffe Square (01865) 277830 open 10am-11.30am 2pm-4.30pm Mon-Sun

Free admission on your own £9.50 for large groups up to 20

The college derives its unusual name from the bronze knocker which hangs above the main door and is said to be shaped like an animal's snout. History tells us that it hung there happily for 100 years until the civil disquiet of the 1300s when it was removed and taken to Lincolnshire by disgruntled students and teachers who finally realised that to get on with their studies they needed a bit of peace and quiet. Having founded a new college there in Stamford, the knocker remained until 1890 when the building came up for sale. Desperate to get its precious snout back, Brasenose purchased the whole building. The original knocker now hangs above the high table in the dining hall.

Brasenose has an enviable position in Radcliffe Square, close to just about everything and in beautiful surroundings. Enter from the High Street and you are in New Quad which branches out into Deer Quad, one of the smallest quads in Oxford and said to be haunted by a cheerful ghost. One guide book claims that the flower bed here is home to the Brasenose tortoise, although having not been seen for the last 13 years, fears about his ill-health are steadily growing. The origin of the Quad's name has two very different stories attached to it. The first suggests it is a dig at Magdalen by calling its smallest quad the Deer Park. The other tells of a Blenheim deer hunt that once ended up all the way in Oxford. The deer, by chance, sought refuge in Brasenose's Chapel, which, despite being God's sanctuary, didn't stop the hounds rushing in and killing it.

The Dining Hall overlooks Old Quad and behind the high table sits the portrait of Alexander Nowell, once the college principle, and said to have invented bottled beer. A keen angler, Nowell used to take beer in bottles on his trips and the fashion caught on. Look behind him on his portrait and you'll see all his fishy paraphernalia. Opposite him sits Betty Morley, the first lady in England to own a watch. You can tell she was proud of the fact as she's holding it in her hand in the portrait.

Deer Quad

Look out also for the statues of the unicorn and lion taken from Brasenose's coat of arms. The unicorn was for many years without its proudest feature until 20 years ago the offending member was replaced for anatomical correctness. This does of course beg the question –

Where was the unicorn's magnificent penis stored all that time??

The college is sometimes unfairly tarnished for being a breeding ground for rugger-buggers and Neanderthal sporty types but this seems a little harsh, as academically it has produced some of the finest PE teachers this country has ever seen.

Heroes and villains

William Golding (author of Lord of the Flies)

John Buchan (author of The 39 Steps)

Jeffery Archer (came here to do a PGCE and although not officially attached to the college in any way he didn't bother to correct anyone who presumed he officially studied here)

Michael Palin (one-time Monty Python member turned intrepid explorer)

Brasenose College Hellfire Club and Brasenose Lane

In the 1820s this notorious club briefly flourished at the college. Not exactly Dead Poets Society, these guys were more interested in vice, drinking, black magic, and general miscreance. One of the more chilling stories about their antics begins just before midnight in Brasenose Lane.

It was around this time that the Vice-Principal of the college, Reverend Churton, was taking a late-night stroll down Brasenose Lane when he noticed a tall man wrapped in a black cloak who seemed to be helping one of the ring-leaders of the club out of his window. The Vice-Principal ran forward, pleased at last to have caught one of them, but as he quickened his pace towards the scene an icy thought went through him and he stopped frozen in his tracks. The student's window (like all the others on the street) was tightly barred and access in or out was impossible. As he approached, in the gloom he could make out the agonised and twisted face of the student as his body was being pulled through the impossibly tight gap of the iron bars.

When the tall man in the black cloak turned to face him, Churton described it as 'the face of pure malevolence and horror' and nothing could have stopped him turning on his heels and fleeing back to the college.

Churton ran all the way to the unfortunate student's room, where he found him lying on the floor, dead, and surrounded by the other wretched-looking members of the group.

The Hellfire club later admitted to having been half-way through a black magic oration when the student started shaking and then dropped dead. Although none of the group would ever confess to the nature or reason for the invocation, they did agree to end the Hellfire Club and it hasn't reared its demonic head in Oxford to this day.

New College

New College

Holywell Street and New College Lane (01865) 279555
Open every day in summer 11am-5pm via New College Lane admission £2, open
Oct-Easter 2pm-4pm Holywell Street admission free

Despite both of its entrances being slightly off the beaten track, New College
is worth tracking down as it is one of the more unusual colleges Oxford has
to offer and at first glance appears to have been built on the ruins of a castle.
Rather than this being the case, the college has in fact been built around a
fair stretch of the old city walls which still have arrow slit features built in.

In New College chapel the disturbing and contorted figure of Lazarus
greets you on the way in and is said to have given Nikita Kruschev a
sleepless night during his visit here in 1958. In contrast, the whole of the
chapel wall at the far end is filled with carved figures, like the lost army of
China, and are in fact a multitude of saints, patriarchal figures and angels.

At the far end, the Garden Quad also has an intriguing feature in the
centre; a large mound (once the burial ground at the time of the Black
Death) which, if you are a
student here or are bold enough,
you can go up and sit at the top
of, and be king of the castle. Ellie
who studied here told me if you
stand in front of the mound and
clap your hands it squeals. I was a
little dubious at first but after a
couple of times discovered it to
be true, it sounds like it's having a
tiny orgasm.

Trivia-wise, the Bond film
'Tomorrow Never Dies' was
briefly filmed here. You know

how in every Bond movie he gets caught on the job somewhere near the beginning of the film and always at the end and usually in a boat?

In this film he's at New College canoodling with some Danish student when his bleeper goes off and M gives the usual *'where the devil are you Bond?'* to which he replies -

'I'm just brushing up on my Danish.'

How can you resist him, girls?

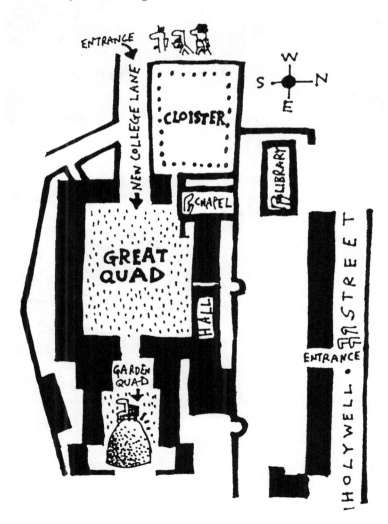

Heroes and villains

Viriginia Woolf (author of 'To the Lighthouse' and the 'Puffin Book of Jokes')

John Fowles (author of the The Collector and The Magus*)

Tony Benn (groovy politician and self-confessed tea-addict, consuming over 40 cups a day!)

Dennis Potter (television playwright whose work included The Singing Detective and Cold Lazarus)

Reverend Spooner (the old warden of New College responsible for inventing Spoonerisms. This is where you get the first syllable of two words the wrong way round which has led to a whole host of 'hilarious' comedy names such as Kenny Everett's Cupid Stunt and Russ Abbott's Friar Tuck)

*I once met someone who came to Oxford to do English literature and in her first term studied The Magus as an example of a failed novel. I read it two years ago and, apart from the pretentious Greek quote at the end, thought it was wonderful. Obviously I need to do the degree to find out where I went wrong.

St John's College

St John's College

(01865) 277300 Open 1pm-5pm Mon-Sun free entry to quads and garden

Notorious for its riches, there is a legend that once you could walk to St John's in Cambridge from St John's in Oxford travelling only on land owned by the two.

The college grounds of St John's hold quite a few surprises for the visitor. Enter the front quad and it will lead you straight onto the college's famous Canterbury quad. I'm not sure whether I happened to mention that I was an expert on Baroque architecture but I have to tell you this is a mighty fine example of it. Some would say that the portals within the logias have enriched entablatures and I'd be inclined to agree with them. Perhaps more importantly the lions and unicorns lazing in the niches of the arches are fun to look out for. St John's most celebrated feature is its gardens, perhaps the finest of all Oxford's colleges and extending all the way from St Giles to Parks Road. With their long lawns, exotic flowerbeds and regal trees, if the sight of a clump of Dizzy Lizzies gives you a secret thrill then these gardens will not disappoint.

If you happen to venture left through the college you'll no doubt stumble across a cocoon of modern buildings serving principally as student accommodation. One part is the Beehive, so-called for its two-storey polygon feature, beyond that is an array of featureless angular buildings linked with a sort of sunken garden theme, except without the garden. Done out in distressing grey concrete it helps serve a reminder that the 70s was a decade of architectural blunders and drug casualties.

Heroes and villains

Kingsley Amis (author of Lucky Jim and father of Martin)

Philip Larkin (poet)

John Wain (the writer not the gunslinger)

Tony Blair (ex-rock musician turned Prime Minister)

Robert Graves (writer)

Jethro Tull (the agricultural reformer not the hairy folk/rock combo)

As well as having a reputation for academic excellence, St John's has its own literary greats, and in the 1950s a writers group called 'The Movement' was led by fellow students Philip Larkin, John Wain and Kingsley Amis. In recent years Amis and Larkin have fallen somewhat out of fashion for their misogynist and rightwing views and of the three, Wain seems best-loved in the town, having written a passionate trilogy charting the struggles of a modern Oxford family.

Tony Blair is another famous person that studied here and by all accounts had a reputation of being something of a ladies man. When he wasn't wooing the ladies he was practising with his rock band 'Ugly Rumour' and prancing about in Cuban heels, medallion and open shirt. I'd give good money for a photo or two.

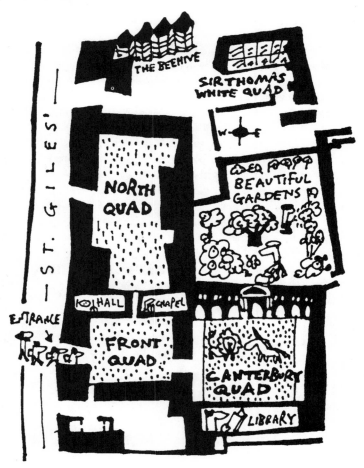

A Guide to Oxford Students

"SPOD"

Spods

Found peeping over huge piles of books in the libraries and lurking around the pool table in the Junior Common Room, Oxford spods are an intelligent but geekish bunch who will undoubtedly get the first they so earnestly work for. Distinguishing features range from bum-fluff facial hair to BO problems, while the more fashion conscious might sport a pair of Wrangler jeans. Perhaps, unsurprisingly, they rarely seem to have partners.

Home

St John's/ Merton/Christ Church/Corpus Christi

Favourite Drug

Cider and real ale

The Lights Are On But Nobody's Home

Despite being another hard-working group, this lot distance themselves from The Spods, partly because they know how to have a good time but mainly because they fail all their exams. Rarely making it past their first year, those that do, often hide their shortcomings behind amateur dramatics, but unfortunately they're lousy actors as well.

Home
Spread thinly throughout most of the colleges

Favourite Drug
Alcopops

The Yawning Majority

Sport, pleasure-seeking and mediocrity are what this lot are about, spending most of their days rowing and having a 'a seriously good time', but always working just enough to keep their tutors happy. In the final year they will, of course, knuckle down, get a 2/1 or 2/2 and go on to get a good job at Arthur Anderson.

Buying into the Oxford myth, the YM will enthusiastically organise the college balls and other events, all the time sporting their college scarves with no sense of irony. Found down the tackiest of Oxford's nightclubs wearing regulation puffa jackets, smart shirts and trousers from Gap.

Home
Exeter/ Worcester/ Jesus/ St Catherine's/ Pembroke/ Teddy Hall and many more.

Favourite Drug
Beer, and lots of it

"THE BEAUTIFUL PEOPLE"

The Beautiful People

Having chosen their college purely for its social status and wealth, these public school oiks from Holland Park see Oxford as utterly beneath their social class and only bothered to venture up here because daddy said it would look good on the CV.

Oxford's social life is of course too provincial for them and they wouldn't be seen dead in any of the clubs here, preferring either to hang out at Freuds or better still in London. Dress code is usually the same as the Yawning Majority, except the jeans are Gucci and the puffa jackets are more expensive. Often to be heard uttering 'ciao baby' or 'cool'.

Home

Magdalen/Oriel/St John's

Favourite Drug

Coke, the powdered variety

"HACK"

Hacks

Politically minded, pompous, obnoxious and universally hated by everyone including each other. Regulation dress usually includes jeans, tucked-in shirt and a tweed jacket. Despite having their sights on being the future Prime Minister, deep down they just need to be loved.

Home
Found loitering around the Oxford Union and OUSU

Favourite Drug
The sound of their own voice

Nerds

Male-only sub-species mainly comprised of frustrated Physics under-graduates sporting fleeces, long hair and a jester hat as some sort of pathetic act of rebellion. Very much the outdoor types, really they're just spods in jugglers clothing who desperately want to be crazy but the only way they know how is to go canoeing at the weekend.

Home
St Anne's/St Catherine's/Wadham/Balliol

Favourite Drug
Vimto/Hi-energy drinks

'NERDS

Slackers

Rich public school boys in combat trousers and with an aversion to deodorant. Slackers spend most of their time sitting in all day, smoking dope and listening to Nick Drake records, rarely venturing out, except to visit their allotments. Common among Law and PPE students, they will happily blow their entire grant on a new stereo or kilo of hash and spend the remainder of term eating nothing but porridge.

Home

Jesus/Keble/Pembroke/Magdalen

Drug

Home-grown (and ketamine for the true professional)

SLACKER

" THE BLAZER BRIGADE"

Brookes students

Tucked away on a hill far, far, far away lies the University formally known as Oxford Poly, occupied by a whole range of social miscreants. One element, The Blazer Brigade, are preppy boys and girls who planned on going to Merton until they found that their A-level in woodwork was not enough, so chose Brookes as a close second. At the other end of the spectrum are the dope-smoking layabouts, similar to the University slackers, except this lot spend most of their time in the pubs on Cowley Road and only ever venture into the city centre to buy specialist rizlas.

Brookes and college students rarely meet and both groups treat each other with extreme suspicion. And while Brookes students definitely have more fun than University students, this is largely due to them not having any real work to do during their time here.

Home

Brookes University and Cowley Road

Drugs

Yes please

Any student who doesn't fit into these categories is merely a figment of your imagination.

DON'T
BREATHE!
BUSES
ARE
FUMING

Shopping

At first sight Oxford doesn't appear to be a haven for much in the way of shopping unless novelty lava lamps, university sweatshirts and inflatable chairs are on your must-have list, but with a little help from our exhaustive shopping exploits, the more intrepid bargain-seeker should find some wonderful places to spend their pocket-money.

Around Carfax the shops are a typical blend of high street chains and tourist traps but once off the beaten track you will be rewarded. Jericho is a good spot for more unique places, try Liscious with its Art-Deco furniture or Little Clarendon Street nearby with its wild array of ethnic artefacts, retro gear and objects for the home. Just off George Street, Gloucester Green has some pretty cool record and clothes shops (not to mention the market here every Thursday), while down at the bottom of The High Street, movie memorablia and packs of Top Trumps can be found from the likes of VinMagCo and Heritage Games.

Perhaps, surprisingly, there are few antique shops considering the number of tourists (especially American) who want to take home something 'authentically English' but have to settle with a packet of digestives and a football. In contrast however, there are a whole host of brilliant bookshops, whose prices, as a rule of thumb, increase according to the amount of dust they contain. Most can be found around The High Street and Broad Street, nestled amongst the giants of Blackwell's and Waterstones but also keep your eyes peeled for the MOMA bookshop and an excellent second hand place in Jericho.

No shopping experience in Oxford however would be truly complete without a trip up the Cowley Road. With its health food shops and last decades New Age fashion boutiques like Bombay Emporium promising 'honestly cheap goods', it could be dismissed purely as a hippy mecca. But in fact the shops here sell everything from skateboards to saris so don't be surprised after an afternoon shopping here to find yourself whizzing home on a new set of roller-blades, wearing a fetching tie-dye suit and clutching a sitar.

BOOK SHOPS

BIG GUYS

Waterstones
Broad Street (01865) 790212

Nestled on the corner of Broad Street and Cornmarket, Waterstones have the sort of location that other shops would happily stick puppies in pies for. I'm glad to say they use their good fortune wisely, with friendly, well-informed staff and three floors of books on every subject you can think of. Also a good spot for the likes of Colin Dexter signing his latest 'Inspector Morse does Debbie from Dallas' epic.

Blackwell's
Broad Street (01865) 792792

Big enough to merit having the very excellent GoodBean café on the first floor. Nothing beats a book and a good cup of coffee (except maybe a play-station and a joint) and you can relax here and read to your heart's desire.

The top floor has a fair selection of second-hand books and they often do great monthly offers on hardback new releases.

Don't miss a quick look in the Norrington room in the basement,

and be ready for a shock. You know how in every Bond film there's a scene where the villain is in his office stroking a cat and he nonchalantly presses a button to reveal a futuristic labyrinth with thousands of workers doing dastardly deeds just behind the bookcase? Well it's sort of like that down here too. It feels like the very nerve-centre of the town. Maybe if these guys' computers go down, all the students would grow mullets, the shark would melt, and Oxford United would score a goal.

Principally this floor is where the students come for their text books but it's definitely worth a visit, especially if you're looking for the history of non-aqueous solvents or need some information on your thesis on Posh Spice.

Also on Broad Street, Blackwell's have another four specialist shops. The Art and Music ones are fairly self-explanatory while Blackwell's Too specialises mainly in children's books. The latest addition to the collection is the Oxford Bookshop which opened in May 2000, selling all things connected with Oxford, from local literary giants to the book in your hand.

LITTLE GUYS

Moma Bookshop
(01865) 201776 Late openings
Thursday during exhibitions. Periodic
student discount

A pricey, but wonderful collection of
experimental literature, 20th century
culture, subculture, art and media.
Everything you need to be part of the
underground intelligentsia is here,
from Bukowski to Derek Jarman,
George Bataille to Dadaism. Also
stocks the occasional art-house
videos and art mags.

Oxfam Bookshop
56 St Giles (01865) 310145

Thirteen years established and still
going strong, Oxfam's first exclusive
bookshop has a fair selection of books
on virtually every topic, and is all the
better in the knowledge that it's for a
good cause. Constantly supplied by a
growing host of donors, Radio 3
presenter Humphrey Carpenter and
the late Iris Murdoch have both given
generously in the past.

Watch out for the stairs at the back
however, many's the time I've been
perusing the history section and nearly
tumbled backwards down the stairs into
the Social Sciences. Remember – good
research can save lives.

Comic Showcase
19/20 St Clements (01865) 723680

Excellent range of comics, with TinTin,
Asterix and Calvin and Hobbes for the
young at heart, to the more serious
collectors' stuff from the likes of Kevin
Smith and Chester Brown. Then
there's Marvel back issues, X-Men, Star
Wars, Pokemon.....

Thornton's
Broad Street (01865) 242939

One of my favourite bookshops in
Oxford. Said to be home to a shy
ghost, this certainly has all the
trappings of a haunted bookshop with
its dusty wooden shelves, windy
staircase and dark corners. According
to Kieran who works there, they often
find customers after-hours, lost in the
sections upstairs. Specialising in Russian
books (including the wonderful
Dictionary of Russian Obscenities) and
Tolkeinalia, they also have a good
selection of other second hand books
that easily merit a visit.

The Little Bookshop
Avenue 2 Indoor Market
(01865) 559176

Run by the charming Philip Gilbert and now in its 24th year, there's plenty for the intrepid book-lover to pour through and a meaty selection of old Penguin classics for only a pound each. This is one of those wonderful topsy-turvy bookshops, which are a pleasure to nose around. Philip is good for a natter about Oxford and life in general, although he's happiest listening to classical music, which he does all day every day. In fact if you can guess what's on Philip's jukebox, he promises to give a discount to anyone discerning enough to know his tastes. And no peeking at his CD collection beforehand, although I know that Bach and Pere Ubu are his current favourites.

Comic Showcase

Jericho Books
48 Walton Street (01865) 511992
www.jerichobooks.com

When so many of the second-hand bookshops in Oxford seem to stock nothing but first edition copies of Jane Austen and obscure 18th century farming manuals, it's good to find a place that makes an effort stocking cult and esoteric stuff. They've got a meaty selection of sci-fi and mind-body-spirit stuff, as well as academic and humanities. In particular, Frank and Sarah know their good stuff from the bad as their knowledge of cool sci-fi authors from Philip K Dick to Kurt Vonnegut goes to show.

The owner was recently murdered in a rather grizzly fashion but it hasn't dampened his spirits much, as it was in a work of fiction. If any of you bookworms out there know the name of the book, drop us a line and you might win a special prize.

> *'nobody ever saw anybody actually open a second-hand bookshop'*
> *Albanian proverb*

The Little Bookshop, in need of a good tidy

RECORD SHOPS

Cornmarket

Mercifully pedestrianised, except for the buses whose sole aim is to reduce the population numbers as efficiently as possible. Good spot for the two main record shops HMV and Virgin.

Massive Records
95 Gloucester Green (01865) 250476 (next to Cult Clothing)

Easy to miss if you weren't paying attention in Gloucester Green,, which if you are a vinyl obsessive Break-Beat fan, would be a shame. Specialising in Hip-Hop, Jungle, Break and other Electronica, this is also a good place to check out related club nights and other events from the fliers or by chatting to the staff, if you can stop them dancing that is.

Avid Records
4 Gloucester Street (just off George Street) (01865) 200411

In case you didn't already know it, vinyl is back, big time. Throw away all your nasty CDs and come back to where big is beautiful and analogue is god. Avid has a meaty collection of used records and is not to be missed by any vinyl lovers. On the first floor you'll find everything from Indie and Heavy Metal to Jazz and ex-chart. Downstairs opens at 1pm where you'll find old Break-Beat, Drum & Bass and Jungle. Their best feature has to be a very meaty collection of 60s and 70s vinyl, in particular Jazz, Soundtrack and Underground Pop. For serious collectors, if you get friendly with the owner you might get to see some of the amazing stuff he's got upstairs, ranging from La Vern Baker to original copies of the Barbarella soundtrack. Last time I was here I joyfully parted company with £20 for an ultra-rare Woody Allen album in perfect condition.

A word of warning! Because of the sheer amount of stuff in the shop, the aisles are incredibly narrow and you'll find yourself having to really squeeze past people as you desperately try and reach the Jazz section in the far corner. So if you're feeling mischievous and want to create a gridlock in a record shop, come on a Saturday and bring a pram and a fat friend.

The Record Fair Town Hall
Monthly £1

If you're looking for modern stuff like Electronica, American Lo-Fi, Post-rock

you in on the best local bands, and where to see good gigs and happily play you the strangest stuff he can get his hands on. Last time I was in he was playing a triple CD musical interpretation of the Tibetan Book of the Dead.

Coming Soon, Shed 7 sings the I Ching.

Something for the Weekend
77 George Street
(01865) 203339

Stocking mags, CDs, drugs paraphernalia and condoms, this is the lifestyle of Human Traffic all rolled into one shop. The name says it all and if you're still into the slightly jaded lifestyle of the lad/drug/club scene this is the place to stock up for a weekend of debauchery. Grab the latest copy of Loaded, some king-sized rizlas, a Cream compilation and a jar of marmite and you have all you need for a night out on the razz.

CLOTHES SHOPS

Queen's Lane is a good place to start for all the predictable clothes shops, with everything from Topshop, Next, New Look, Burton, French Connection, Gap and not forgetting Millets. For your slightly more up-market ladies shops, you'll find Oasis, Monsoon and Karen

or strange Break-Beat, forget it, the weirdest thing you'll find here is Stereolab. If you're just on the look-out for some 60s vinyl or CDs at knock-down prices you'll probably be happy. There's a good selection of Rock and Pop, especially rare Indie from the 80s and 90s. There's even a modest selection of Jazz and Soul. If you don't find anything worth buying though, you still might feel a little bit cheated after paying a quid to get in.

The Polar Bear
183 Cowley Road
(01865) 251443

Stocking a nifty selection of new and used CDs, this is the place not only to pick up some cool bargains but also to get a feel for the music scene in Oxford. The two sections to look out for must be their 'top used CD bargain' section and '60 great albums for under a tenner.' They also have a great selection of local music including Peel favourites Shifty Disco and the likes of Bigger the God.

The staff are lovely, Michael will fill

Millen in St Ebbes, and Jigsaw, Coast, Phase 8 and Whistles all at the top of the High street near Carfax Tower. For men I'm afraid the story's not so good. The conservative clothes shops (of which there are many) will want to dress you up like Stephen Fry, while the painfully hip ones go more for the full on Techno-kid come Ali G look. True, there are a few good second-hand shops but beyond that you're struggling and you might have to try a place down the road I know called London.

Oslo Tuft
21 High Street (01865) 248796

After the initial lack of success with their earlier shops Copenhagen Clump and Stockholm Sod, they seem to have finally hit a winning formula with this one. The more discerning Post-Rock, Nu-Skate, Big-Beat gentleman can find gear from the likes of Stussy, Camper, Paul Smith, and Denime.

DNA
1-3 St Michael's Street (01865) 790568

Trendy clothes for you chic young things. Nothing out of the ordinary in their stock except a pair of jeans hanging on the wall, said to have once been owned by Orson Welles in his later years.

SS20
131 Cowley Road (01865) 791851
www.ss20.com

Cool little skateboarding shop selling hats, videos, clothes and other skate gear. It's not cheap but then you can hardly go out skateboarding in C&A gear can you? They also do board hire.

Footprints
High Street and Gloucester Green (01865) 725133

Slightly unusual collection of shoes and boots, ranging from DMs, biker boots and Caterpillar to cowboy boots and a modest selection of kinky boots for the ladies. Generally the kind of stuff when you were a teenager your mum would have despaired at and said –

'young lady, what have you got on your feet?' Then you would have a tutting fit, roll your eyes, pop your chewing gum a couple of times and go to your bedroom to dream about marrying David Soul.

Oxford Boot Store and Maximillions
11 Avenue1, Covered Market (01865) 249531

Describing themselves as the Jekyll

His best feature is that if you yell 'Yee Haaw' from the other side of the shop, he'll tell you the best joke I've ever heard.

Seed
14 St Clements (01865) 201777
www.seed-company.co.uk

Found next to Club Latino, near Magdalen Bridge, Seed describes itself as a Concept Salon, which I took to mean they'd cut your hair with a theme in mind, say sci-fi, or Period Drama, but it simply means they do hair and sell clothes as well.

They've currently got a modest selection of stuff from the likes of Bloggs, Lambretta, Pash and Ice Kube, as well as some pretty cool chunky jewellery. Trendy without being pretentious, friendly owner Grange is a serious clubber, so last time I was in I asked what he thought of Club Latino next door.

'Yeah, right! I've never even seen inside it mate, except when my builder fell through the floor last year.'

Cult Clothing
Gloucester Green (01865) 794454

Probably the biggest fashionable clothes shop in Oxford and certainly the most established, with tons of big label names and a heavy slant towards club-wear and street fashion for all you budding Fatboyslim's. If you can't afford their prices but still want something hip to wear for an evening 'largin' it in Oxford, then the sale shop up the road in Friar's Entry sells their cut-price stuff.

and Hyde of footwear, Maximillian is the Dr Jekyll, a no-nonsense shoe shop, while the Oxford Boot store, our Mr Hyde, is where our sinister story lies.

Selling a mix of outdoor footwear ranging from DMs to American cowboy boots, the owner, after a visit to Denver two years ago, decided to liven the place up by investing in two mechanical cowboys. JC stands in the window torturing the staff with his monotonously tapping stick, while Gabby, a full-sized cowboy, sits in a chair by the till and sings and tells stories to the customers. He's very friendly but his eyes do remind me of those old Scooby Doo cartoons where the evil caretaker in the old castle would watch Shaggy and co from behind a painting.

2ⁿᵈ-HAND CLOTHES

The Bead Games Shop
40 Cowley Road (01865) 251620

Taking its name from the Herman Hesse novel, this is something of an Alladin's cave and reminds me of the clothes shop in Mr Ben. Try on one of their fake leopard-skin coats and you might mysteriously find yourself on a jungle adventure.

Beyond doubt this has to be the most interesting and flamboyant collection of second-hand and new clothes anywhere in Oxford. Expect to find anything from corsets, basques, French lingerie, Kameez, PVC, fake fur, jewelled trousers, hand-knitted jumpers and even traditional peasants' jackets. Sorry guys, it's mostly for the girls, you'll have to make do with the terribly exciting collection of jeans and jumpers from Gap again, I'm afraid. Its rather eccentric owner Erica also makes clothes out of old velvet curtains and saris as well as doing a neat line in bizarre and silly postcards, French brollies and wands. I guess I should also mention that she sells beads.

Revival Clothes Agency
60 St Clements (01865) 251005

Run by Heather and Elaine, the shop sells a fair selection of contemporary second-hand clothes in good nick. There's more choice for women than men, and much of the stock seems for the more conservative lady, but if you take the time to look around you might find something a bit daring. For men there are some cheap suits and

DJs in the basement. Levis generally go for around £18.

Uncle Sams
25 Little Clarendon Street (01865) 510759

A gem of a place for the second-hand clothes-shopper and lover of vintage 60s/ 70s gear. Be an extra from The Sweeney, Modesty Blaize or the sitar player in Kula Shaker within 5 minutes. The range of stock is fantastic, especially for shirts and coats. They also have a sprinkling of second-hand furniture alongside the Duffle coats at the back. Leather jackets and jeans are still their best sellers, it's good to know the spirit of The Fonz is alive and well with the good citizens of Oxford.

Sit on it.

Unicorn
Ship Street

One of the strangest second-hand clothes shop I've ever visited. Operating on the policy of, 'the more the merrier', in terms of stock, the shop is now so full of clothing that actually getting into the shop is becoming a struggle, never mind trying to have a look at anything. Mix that with the gloomy lighting in here and you have a recipe for disaster.

Every time I go in, the owner is trying to have a clear out, but ten years down the line and, if anything, it's getting worse. But I offer these humble opinions out of love and look forward to the day the back room is liberated once again so I can have a nose around the suits and jackets.

COOL THINGS FOR THE HOME
Little Clarendon Street

The best place to start without a shadow of a doubt. Not only a bohemian denizen of coffee-houses and restaurants, but Little Clarendon Street (or Elsie as it's known) also doubles as a place to buy stylish furniture, household items and other natty things for the home.

Ottoman specialise in coffee-table culture for men, with various stylish items in chrome and plastic but also a few oddities such as model scooters for Mr thirty-something-used-to-be-a-Mod-but-now-drives-a-BMW, and the kind of books you pick up but never buy. Up from there is **Sylvester's**, yet another one of those novelty item shops, which stocks the usual array of funny shaped clocks and lava lamps (surely everyone's bought one by now?).

Did they really have a T-shirt in the window that had *'All this and my dad's loaded'* scrawled across the chest?

Who buys this stuff?

If Habitat is a notch up from Ikea, then **Central** is a notch above Habitat (see diagram). This independent shop stocks a lovely range of stylish modern furniture, kitchenware, gadgets and objet d'art, and is the sort of place where it's all too easy to blow a ton of cash you weren't expecting to. Nice range of

Ladder of sophistication

LISCIOUS
CENTRAL
HABITAT
IKEA
EDINBURGH WOOL SHOP

leather chairs and sofas too if you can afford them.

If ethnic stuff is more your bag there's **Tumi** at the top, where you can kit yourself out like the pan-pipe band from the Fast Show, or **Oriental Crafts** lower down, with a selection of Eastern paraphernalia and notably some rather lovely Chinese crockery and soup bowls.

Central 33-35 Little Clarendon Street (01865)511700
Oriental Crafts (keep your nose peeled for the smell of incense)
Ottoman 31 Little Clarendon Street (01865)311393
(Open Mon-Sat 9.30am-6pm Sun 11.30am-5.30pm)
Sylvester (you can't miss it, unfortunately)
Tumi (listen out for the panpipe music)

Park End Antiques and Interiors, Casablanca and Dada to Rara
10 Park End Street
(01865) 2000091/ 717291

For lovers of quality antique furniture, Art Deco lights and plenty more besides, Park End antiques may be a little off the beaten track but is well worth the visit.

Inside there are several stalls selling different antiques from clothes to objets d'art. Casablanca is run by Penny and is a collection of 30s clothing, feather boas and jewellery, and although primarily for the female of the species, seems to cater for a thriving transvestite and velvet fetishist market too.

Nick in Dada to Rara has a nifty selection of 50s and Art Deco furniture as well as stuff like sci-fi style lamps, glass cool tables and chrome chairs. He's also good for a natter about nothing in particular and will accept yen as hard currency.
With the ever-looming threat of more chain cafés and restaurants in Oxford, places like this deserve all the support you can give them.

St Clements Antiques
93 St Clements (01865) 727010

Run by the mildly eccentric Giles Power and specialising in the more 'bizarre and unusual' antiques, this is a collection of curiosities, ranging from clockwork spits to Giles himself. On entering, visitors instantly relinquish all rights to leave empty handed unless they agree to partake in a number of fruitless games, all made up by Giles himself to wile away the hours.

The Antiques Gameshow
with your host Giles Scully
The rules are very simple…
1) Examine every item in the shop carefully. Applying what scant knowledge you have of antiques, try and guess the oldest thing in the room. If you do you instantly win a 20% discount.
2) Play **'What the Hell is that?'**, loosely based on the TV show of the same name, where Giles presents you with a strange object and you have to decide whether it's:
a) a device for extracting bees milk,
b) a medieval torture implement for pigs.
c) a coat-stand for dwarves.
Anyone who answers correctly wins....20% discount.
3) The shop record (held by Giles) for playing Bilboquet is 8. Beat it and, you guessed it, that 20% discount could be yours.

Liscious
102 Walton Street
(01865) 552232/ (0973) 479057

Run by Fran with a sexy voice, and her butler Walter, Liscious specialise in post 1920s lighting, Art Deco furniture

and chairs that wouldn't look out of place on a James Bond set. In fact the last time we were in, Thom Yorke had just bought the chair in the photo below (that's his fresh bum print you can see). Run by a lovely couple with an eye for beautiful objects, some of the more unusual stuff might break the bank for some of you, but if you're down on your luck you can still buy a 1930s crêpe de chine handkerchief for 100p*.

Oxford Forum of Ancient Art
3 North Parade Avenue (01865) 316366

Out of town, just off the Banbury road, this shop sells ancient yet authentic artefacts from the likes of the Roman Empire and the Ming Dynasty. With stock ranging from vases, plates, statues and jewelry, don't expect them to be giving the stuff

away (some of it is over two thousand years old) but they do all come with a certificate of authenticity. But to be certain it isn't a fake, make sure you get a certificate of authenticity for the certificate of authenticity. And then you'll need a certificate of authenticity for the certificate of authenticity for the certificate of ......

The Oxford Gallery
23 High Street (01865) 242731

Situated towards the top of the High Street, the Oxford Gallery has been open for 32 years and, surprisingly, is one of only a small handful of galleries in the city. They are particularly well known for their jugs, pots, mugs, jewellery and other nice things that aren't paintings. In saying that, they also have a gallery downstairs which has constant exhibitions, sometimes of very famous works (we saw a Picasso but are still convinced it was a print from Athena). The cheapest thing you can buy is roughly a tenner. If you have 20 grand you can go a bit more upmarket.

*An extra 50p if you want Thom's bogies on it.

Oxford Holographics
71 High Street (01865) 250505

Still known locally as the hologram shop as for many years in the 80s and early 90s that was pretty much all they sold, until the damned things mercifully went out of fashion. Despite a few still desperately lingering around on the walls, OH is now crammed with every gadget, gizmo, ethnic craft and modern tat you can think of, from lava lamps to millennium mouse-mats. Yes Oxford is full of these kind of shops, but I suppose OH deserves a mention for being there first. The question is- do we thank them or curse them for it?

Antiques on High
85 High Street (01865) 251075
Discounts available on cash purchases

Having moved from the old Jam factory, they obviously have an affinity for breakfast condiments as their new premises used to be the offices for an old marmalade factory. Inside, it is surprisingly large, stocking over 30 different stalls and cabinets of different antiques ranging from watches, jewellery and books to ceramics.

Look out for Mick with his Arthur Scargill haircut, and if you have a stuffed badger please sell it to Andy as he is plagued by a tiny woman who visits him on a regular basis asking for one.

Oddest customer request goes to the man who came in last year and had 3 bullets dug out of his chest and had them mounted on a chain around his neck.

ODDITIES

VinMagCo
50 High Street (01865) 240859

A haven for movie buffs, music lovers and fans of the glamour of yesteryear, this shop stocks everything from photos of your favourite actors to movie posters, models, toys, books and T-shirts. Stock ranges from the 70s cheese of Hammer Horror and Starsky and Hutch to the 50s sophistication of Cary Grant. You can even purchase copies of the birth certificates of your rock idols: Lennon, Macca, Bowie and err..Peter Cushing.

My favourite items in the shop (apart from their Incredible Hulk mouse-mats) have to be these authentic looking model 'Clangers' for £15, which look divine on the mantle piece. Not only that but they also do a pretty good line in Bagpuss and Professor Yaffle.

The owner promises to be opening another shop in Oxford soon, specialising in authentic old movie posters.

It's interesting to note that mediocre and mindless girl and boy bands may rule the airwaves but the most popular idols (according to the guy working here) are still Audrey Hepburn and Sean Connery. Step aside Geri Halliwell and Liam Gallagher, there's hope for us yet.

Heritage Games
72 High St
(01865) 203244
www.heritagegames.co.uk

A cool selection of games with around 500 to choose from. The bestsellers are all there; Monopoly, Risk and Top Trumps. Also, keep an eye open for the Elvis playing cards and a good selection of those murder mystery games which give you an excuse to dress up as a nurse for the evening.

The Chocolate Shop
63 Cowley Road

Very bizarre. From the outside this shop doesn't appear to sell anything or be open, as the window only contains empty Twix boxes. But look carefully and you'll spot the old guy in there. On entering it feels like walking into a time bubble from the 1970s but don't get your hopes up for chocolate, all he's got is a handful of penny chews and a few old stamps.

It's quite sad really, the owner probably can't afford to buy in any more stock so do me a favour, if you go in, promise you'll buy something.

Even if it's a few old Venezuelan stamps that you didn't really want, you'll be doing your good deed for the day.

The Fishbowl
118-122 Magdalen Road
(01865) 241825

A paradise for fish-lovers or anyone wanting to take home their partner an exotic fish-dish for their supper. It's a wonderful feeling losing yourself in their endless corridors of strange and beautiful fish and they've got everything from piranhas and tiny sharks to marine invertebrates, lobsters, coral and eels. They even used to stock octopi but the owner told me they'd keep climbing out of their tanks and scaring the children.

The Annual Cheeky Aquatic Creatures Awards
Sponsored by Trill

Most expensive fish
Red Arowanna, at £3,600
The dullest-looking fish
Red Arowanna
Ugliest fish
South American Catfish
(It looks like a kind of fat, ugly Salvador Dali)
Silliest fish
Bubble Eyed fish
(The Marty Feldman of the fish world)
Cutest fish
Striped damsels
(Looks like a Humbug with fins)

"Tickling urchins on a Saturday morning is a great thing to do."

Magdalen street resident

MARKETS

Gloucester Green Market
Every Thurs 8am-4pm but they do start to clear away early sometimes. Most popular in summer months

Arts, crafts, collectables and antiques can all be found here. Delve further into the rows of stalls and you'll discover a world of hippy clothes, picture frames, boots, old prints, rugs and throws, candles, light shades, crockery and second hand books. If you are not interested in all of that then wander around listening to the owners of the stalls. I overheard one bloke trying to sell a dinner set....

'yeh, 23 carat gold that luv, German construction, pre-First World War, Adolf Hitler used it, nice bloke, not a scratch, normally 900 quid. For you darlin, 20. Can't do better than that'.

You can pick something up here for as little as £3 (army clothes) or as much as £200 (antique jewellery). A bargain is always round the corner. One very friendly stall owner, Pat, gets a mention for demonstrating her antique box that gives the user an electric shock. I just got out of hospital last week.

Northgate Antiques
Cornmarket Street
Open 9am-5pm Mon-Fri

Mercifully hidden down an alleyway next to St Michael's Church on Cornmarket, this has to be the saddest collection of worthless tat I've ever set my eyes on, and what's worse they have the cheek to charge 20p for the privilege of a 30 second perusal. Expect Charles and Di cups, Victorian postcards and piles of cheap novels from the 80s bargain bucket. I can only imagine it survives on its 20ps from desperate passers-by avoiding unexpected downpours on Cornmarket.

The Indoor Market
High Street & Cornmarket

Set up many years ago to relieve congestion of traders on the main road, the market is a strange mix of old-style cafés, bookshops, heelers, butchers, florists and fish stalls juxtaposed with modern clothes shops, shoe shops and gift shops. It's well worth spending some time idling your way through the aisles here as there are some interesting shops to see, (especially the old bookshop), and if you get peckish you can always grab a snack at Georgina's Café. The time to see the market at its best must surely be at Christmas when the butchers hang the turkeys, chickens, wild boar and other festive meats up and you feel like you're walking around in some Dickensian Christmas tale.

COSTUME RENTAL & PARTY SHOPS

Party Mania

179 Kingston Road (01865) 513397

If you keep following Walton Street deep into Jericho, you'll find this wonderful place. The shop has a good selection of costumes for hire and every novelty joke item you can think of, from remote-controlled fart machines, to penis pasta.

Dominated by the larger-than-life personalities of Mary and Nicki, who are rather like Mrs Slocombe and Margo from the Good Life all rolled into one, they spend the day sharing their saucy humour and bizarre anecdotes with the customers.

Apart from the predictable mass of blokes buying fake breasts for their mate's stag do, the customers also include many of Oxford's white witches, who usually hire medieval gear for ceremonies.

Oxford's resident werewolf is also known to pop in at times to buy rubber chickens and other essential werewolf items. Mary said -

'he's got the typical one eyebrow, hairy face and sunken forehead. When he first came in, he tried to convince us he was a werewolf, and we didn't believe him. But since his stories about the things he got up to in the caves in Wooton-Under-Edge, he really has got us all wondering…'

And before you think it, it can't be Gaz from Supergrass because he lives in Brighton now.

Other famous customers include Jeremy Irons, spotted buying Christmas crackers, and Richard Branson who got a pair of novelty 'glow in the dark' handcuffs.

When I was last in here, the hundredth bloke of the day was rather shyly purchasing a pair of novelty breasts, so Mary considerately gave him a see-through bag to carry them home in. Now there's a woman after my own heart.

The Ballroom
5-6 The Plain
(01865) 202303/ 241054

When the near-legendary Sweet Charity outgrew its home on Cowley Road, the owner simply lifted up her cocktail dress and ran around the corner to bigger premises. Run by a handful of charming ladies, this is the place to go if you're off to a ball or fancy something different for a night down DTM. Stocking the usual array of DJs, other formal wear for men, and over 3000 dresses for the ladies, it doesn't, however, stop there. For the more adventurous there are Lord Byron-style frilly shirts, Spats, gangster suits, Austin Powers costumes and several gimp outfits. Prices for hire are reasonable and upstairs you'll find a modest selection of used suits, velvet jackets and cocktail dresses for the less affluent. Be warned however, if you get involved in a food fight and lose, expect to be handed a hefty bill for cleaning.

The ladies from Partymania prepare for another gruelling day selling chocolate willies and fake breasts

Celebrations
Market St
(01865) 202608

Good selection of fancy dress, party stuff, jokes and other novelty items. You may be perturbed to know that the most popular costumes for hire are currently Mr Blobby and the Teletubbies, although for copyright reasons theirs are called Fat Mr Pinky and the Portly Television Creatures, or something like that. Students flock here in their multitude for the tradition of giving balloons and flowers as post exam gifts, and for the Mayday festival they also specialise in novelty phalluses, which students strap onto their legs in honour of Mayday's more exotic pagan traditions.

My favourite item in the shop has to be the horribly delicious jelly severed fingers and toes.

Claire who works there said-

'People come in expecting to shock me by asking for things like rubber chickens and furry handcuffs but it's nothing unusual to me. Saying that, someone recently asked for a cock-ring, and that did make me blush.'

I took that as a challenge, and hope you'll do likewise.

A cheeky tale

After a hard day's reviewing with my faithful sidekick Dippy we popped into The Ballroom at the end of the day to pick up some photos and somehow got talking about sheet music. Before I knew it, out of the blue and tired with reviewing all day, Dippy found himself repeating to the owner that old Russ Abbott standard –

'Sheet music? No it's really good, actually.'

The owner looked at us both with utter contempt and shaking her head said –

'You're writing the Cheeky Guide to Oxford, and that's the best you could come up with? Lord help us ...'

Food

Catering for your wildest culinary delights and more besides, Oxford has a reputation for some excellent curry-houses, a diverse selection of Mediterranean and modern continental restaurants, and over 30,000 pubs in the city-centre all serving traditional microwave lasagne.

Try some of the cafés and restaurants on The High Street for a touch of sophistication, or the Jamaican place HiLo and some of the Indian restaurants on the Cowley Road at the weekends for a full-on party atmosphere and great food. There really is a wonderfully rich choice of places to eat on offer in Oxford but despite all this, McDonalds still seems the most popular destination for visitors. If only the likes of the Grand Café and the Old Parsonage gave away free plastic Star Wars figures with their yak's cheese salad and crème brûlée we wouldn't have this problem.

Not being ones for star ratings, the restaurants reviewed here are mainly ones that we like eating at, have a good reputation, or happen to be run by members of our family. For the penny-conscious and miserly we have included a simple cash rating as when you're on a tight budget it's nice to know where you can get a meal for under a fiver that isn't a stale burger. All restaurants reviewed have veggie options.

Budget = £0-5 per person
Moderate = £5-10 per person
Expensive = £10 plus per person

FOOD

CENTRAL CAFÉS

Café Boheme
73 High Street (01865) 245858
Open 8am-1am and weekends 9am-2am (at the manager's discretion)
Sunday 9am-11pm
Moderate

Situated towards the lower end of the High Street and part of the Westgate Hotel, Café Boheme has added to the increasing number of posh wine bar, brasserie type-places along this main thoroughfare. It is spacious, comfortable, relaxed and amazingly, for a French café, actually has French waitresses, so swear loudly in French, to test how French they are (it's not easy to get the word French in a sentence four times).

Entertainment-wise, from 4pm-6pm, Mondays to Thursdays, they do live Jazz and the resident piano has its ivories plunked. If you hate Jazz, take ear plugs with you and watch 'Hardy & Laurel' films (as we were told*) on the big screen.

The food here is wonderful and plentiful, coming served on huge plates. Seafood fans will not be disappointed as they do everything from scallops, squid and salmon to swordfish. As well as typical French dishes it's even a place you can bring your stereotypical Northern parents, as steak and Cumberland Sausages are also on the menu.

An evening main course, bottle of wine and water cost around £20 but alternatively you could pop in for

their kipper breakfast. If that still breaks the bank then just come here for a cocktail or coffee and enjoy the surroundings.

Georgina's
Avenue 3, Indoor Market High Street (01865) 249527
Open Mon-Sat 8am-5pm
Moderate

Decorated with bright colours, bamboo blinds, Toulouse Lautrec's on the walls and movie posters stuck on the low ceilings, there's no mistaking this as a student hang-out. Far from tacky though, Georgina's is in fact an intimate place with plenty of character and the likes of Neil Young strumming away in the background.

Like all good cafés, breakfast is served all day and they do a good range of bagels, omelettes and baguettes with some excellent fillings, try the brie and fresh mango or the spicy Mexican chicken.

Not cheap, (a baguette and juice for two will come to over £10), this is a place to meet friends, have a natter, and see how long you can make your drink last before it evaporates..

GoodBean Café
First floor of Blackwell's Bookshop
50 Broad Street (01865) 727147
Mon-Sat 9am-6pm except Tuesday 9.30am start, Sun 11pm-5pm
Moderate

Although they don't shout about it (which I think they should) GoodBean have some impressive

*in fact it was 'Wise & Morcambe'

A Brasenose couple puzzle over some long words in Hello magazine at Georgina's Café

policies for their food which means that all their produce is GM free, eggs are free-range, the tuna is dolphin-friendly, the meat is RSPCA approved.* and you can even have soya milk with your coffee.

Situated on the first floor of Blackwell's the aroma of coffee has been a welcome addition to the bookshop enticing many a bookworm to snuggle down with a drink and one of the books off the bookshelf up there.

Priding themselves on making 'damn fine coffee', GoodBean probably also do the best hot chocolate in Oxford (made of real Belgian chocolate chunks) as well as an imaginative selection of sandwiches including my favourite, turkey and cranberry, which they don't just save for Christmas.

The atmosphere is always relaxed and friendly in there and being situated in the heaving metropolis that is Broad Street, GoodBean is particularly welcome news to any weary visitors, who after being subjected to the horrors of the Oxford Story will find solace in a coffee and Danish pastry.

classiest café. The food fits the surroundings in terms of price and style, and as well as salads and sandwiches for lunch they do a wonderful afternoon cream tea and tapas in the evening. For drinks you can choose from fresh coffee, tea, cocktails, beer, wine and soft drinks to wash it all away.

They claim to be on the site of the first coffee house in England (1650) and to celebrate its antiquity have Milton quotes on the wall which are the only thing that somehow spoil the decadent charm of the place. Well worth a visit in the evening, even if just to slurp your way through a Baileys latte or to sample their delicious chocolates.

The Grand Café
84 High Street (01865) 204463
Open 9am-11pm
Afternoon cream teas. 3.30pm-6pm
Expensive

A cross between Buckingham Palace and Rick's bar in Casablanca this is a definite contender for Oxford's

MOMA Café
30 Pembroke Street (01865) 813814
Open 9.30am-5.30pm Tue-Sat
Thurs-9am-9pm Sun 11am-5.30pm
Budget

You'll find this place deep in the basement of the MOMA. The food

*That doesn't mean they make unwanted pets into sandwiches

is inexpensive and there's a fair range of veggie stuff as well as a mean chicken pie and a good choice of delicious cake. Seating-wise I'd avoid the tables by the wall if you can as they're a bit low for eating on; they're more for lounging around, sipping coffee and discussing the latest Rolf Harris exhibition upstairs (but they may be your only choice on a busy day).

Unspoiled with musak, this café has an informal, friendly feel to it and my only concern is that the carpet somehow reminds me of my Primary school days, sat cross legged on the floor reciting my three times table. Top marks however for the cinnamon, nutmeg and chocolate shakers. Nice touch.

The Nosebag
6-8 St Michael's Street
(01865) 721033 Open 9.30am-5.30pm
Mon, 9.30am-10pm Tues -Fri, 9.30pm
-10.30pm Fri-Sat 9.30am-9pm Sun*
Moderate

I can't decide who's grumpier here, the staff or the customers. Every time I come in someone is having a moan about something. This is a slightly up-market version of Binns Café complete with all the whinge-bags you'd normally find there. They do counter service, however, so if Meltz next door is packed and you're feeling peckish you might find yourself in here in a moment of desperation.

*except leap years when the opening times are equal to the sum of the square of the hypotenuse.... I don't know, why can't they just have sensible opening times instead of all this shenanigans.

If Victor Meldew came to Oxford he'd eat here.

Queen's Lane Coffee House
40 High Street (01865) 240082
Open 8am-8pm Mon-Sat, 9am-7pm
Sun
Moderate

This unspoiled small coffee house half way up the High Street is set in the heart of student land, and is in fact one of only several thousand coffee houses claiming to be the oldest in Britain, nay, Europe. The café proudly wears its history on its sleeves, or walls to be exact, as you can read about its checkered past as you tuck into your sandwich, but try not to be put off by their colour scheme of salmon and pale mushy pea green.

The food here is reasonably priced with plenty of tempting cuisine. I recommend coming here for late breakfast, as the choice is good and it's the perfect time to soak up that academic vibe as hairy faced men pour over books with no pictures in, and girls in cardigans agonise over what to wear for their staircase ball.

COWLEY ROAD CAFES

Café Coco
Cowley Road (01865) 200232
Open 10am-11pm Mon-Sun
Moderate

This Mediterranean-style café at the bottom of Cowley Road has a sort of French-colonial flavour to its design and food, and is a very popular haunt for the Cowley Road student population and locals.

The food is good, with generous portions, but after eating here a few times I do find the choice a bit limited, as the menu mainly consists of pizzas, fish and salad. What it may lack in variety, however, the café more than makes up for in style.

You'd be hard pushed not to notice the clown sat in the bath at the back of the room and the 'Brazil' style vents, while in the middle is a Cheer's-type bar for anyone just dropping by for a drink to sit at.

At night it gets very busy and the atmosphere is very welcoming but if you don't like smoky cafés then beware, it seems that sometimes the whole of Cowley Road descend here just to have a fag.

The Excelsior Café
Cowley Road (01865) 248504
8am-5pm Mon-Sun
Budget

Come enter the strange and frightening world of the Excelsior Café, a cross between Twin Peaks and a Mike Leigh film. The café's winning formula seems to be based on its ambience of mystique provided by a dense cloud of cigarette smoke while piped music has been replaced in favour of the sound of hacking coughs. And while the manager glides slowly around the room taking orders in his deadpan Boris Karloff voice, the other customers in the café sit motionless, staring at you with vacant eyes.

EXCELSIOR CAFÉ

Although the menu includes such delights as Horlicks, spaghetti and chips, jelly and ice-cream, this is essentially a place to come for that hangover-cure greasy spoon breakfast but don't try asking for anything fancy. Last time I was in I asked for the breakfast without beans and my girlfriend wanted her eggs sunny side down and no tomatoes. The waiter stared at us, wrote nothing down, and when our food arrived we just got two standard breakfasts.

If you like an element of surrealism and horror with your eating experiences, this is the real McCoy. And make sure to ask for their Arabic Cannon and Ball mug for your coffee.

Joe's Café
21 Cowley Road. (01865) 201120
Open 11am-11pm Mon-Fri, 10am-11pm weekends
Moderate

Once called Joey's, this cramped and popular café provides a meaty transatlantic repertoire. It's very friendly and is particularly well known for its hearty burgers and chunky breakfasts. You will walk out of Joe's very full so make sure a taxi is waiting to whisk you straight home without the need to walk anywhere. There's normally a healthy serving of students here, often entertaining their parents in a bid to negotiate more pocket money.

They also do good cocktails and have a tiny garden in which to stand around stripping. *

*typing error, I meant sipping

JERICHO CAFÉS

The Jericho Café
112 Walton Street (01865) 310840
Mon-Thurs 8am-10.30pm Fri & Sat
8am-11pm Sun 9am-6pm
Moderate

Welcoming, eight-year-old North Oxford café with a good selection of salads, Mediterranean food and sandwiches (to take away or eat in).

Keep an eye on the board for the day's specials as they can often be quite tempting and if you fancy dropping by for breakfast not only is the choice good but this is a perfect café to lounge around in and read the morning papers. The downstairs area can be quiet and intimate for those who like such things while the notice board, on the way down, is useful for catching up with local goings on. Find out who to call to get your cat neutered or where to do a spot of Brazilian dancing. And if you get bored of the music, they'll even let you put on your own CD.

Café Something
30 Walton Street (01865) 559782
Open 8am-7pm Mon-Fri, 9am-7pm
Sat, 10am-7pm Sun
Budget

An airy, cheap and cheerful café with a relaxing atmosphere to boot. This is a student haunt and as such they get the privilege of hanging their artwork on the walls. The 'cheapest breakfasts in Oxford' come in seven choices

and range from £3 to £6. There are also plans to create a lounge area and an internet cyber section downstairs.

George & Davis
55 Little Clarendon Street
8am-12pm everyday
Budget

Oxford's very own ice-cream parlour offering a range of delicious flavours with new ones being created every week. In fact if a flavour of your choice obtains 30 signatures, it is made into the real thing. There are some great potentials, including gin & tonic sorbet, carrot cake, pear & champagne, Pimms and, my favourite; rotten leaf flavour.

The customer participation continues on Monday nights, when, if you throw a cow into the basketball hoop, a large pile of ice cream is yours for the taking. While on Tuesday evenings you receive a 20% discount if you actually bring along a real cow!

Incredibly popular and the downfall of many of a diet.

The Beat Café
Little Clarendon Street (see veggie
and organic restaurants)

Freud
119 Walton Street (see cocktail
bars)

JAMAICAN

HiLo

68-70 Cowley Road,
(01865) 725984
Opening times are erratic at the best
of times, but it's always open late
Moderate

Far, far away from the mundane world, in a universe all of its own sits HiLo, a Jamaican restaurant come late-night-drinking-den and the heart-beat of Cowley Road.

Poles apart from much of Oxford's more formal, conservative restaurants, HiLo seems to open and close when it feels like it, there is no set menu, and legend dictates that you are charged on what they think you can afford.

The food is typically Caribbean with red snapper and Jerk chicken

as main courses and sweet potato, breadfruit and plantain for starters.

The service is slow, so relax yourself into a full night ahead and take advantage of their selection of Jamaican beers.

Come here at the weekend and you'll discover that HiLo is the fantastic party that all your life you suspected was going on somewhere else but no one had invited you. Open until the small hours, it is usually packed with students, Cowley Road locals and Rastas, and is very popular for late-night drinking (provided you buy a popadom). During the week it's a little quieter but you can expect to be entertained by the owners, who specialise in Jamaican glove-puppet theatre.

The décor inside is wonderfully ramshackle, it always looks like they're half-way through moving in, with boxes of yams lying around, paintings sitting on the floor and the rather alarming maritime toilets that, at weekends, look like they've been through a storm at sea.

For an unforgettable evening, come here early on a Friday night and you will wake up Saturday morning and swear it was just a dream.

I came here one night, with some newly acquainted friends, with the intention of reviewing the place rather than getting wildly drunk but unfortunately succumbed to the latter, forgot all about reviewing, and the only thing that made it into my note-book was – 'scrotum sack lighting'. If you visit and drink enough beer you'll understand.

Tip – if you're eating, dress down for the occasion, it'll be cheaper.

Beat Café
Little Clarendon Street
(01865) 553543
Open 10am-11pm Mon-Sat, 10am-10.30pm Sun
Moderate

This family-run café/bar has to be one of the most strikingly decorated in Oxford. Nestled discreetly at the top of Little Clarendon Street, at first glance only the stained glass windows give an inkling of what is to come, until you step inside. The interior is decorated in a dark Egyptian theme, with psychedelic fans and expansive, weird National Geographic photos that bear down on you from the walls. Downstairs is equally mysterious with its framed Buddha set deep into the wall, and beautiful lighting

Downstairs at the Beat Café..........hang on a minute, isn't that a Jazz Album?

effects, all dreamed up and designed by one of the brothers.

The food is imaginative, healthy and well-presented vegetarian. The choice ranges from Tempura vegetables, stuffed mushrooms and soya burgers to some marvellous puddings. They've even got cigarettes in their menu with everything from Gitanes to the essential Marlboro lights.

The restaurant may look like Kenneth Anger let loose on Changing Rooms, but the clientele definitely aren't beatniks. Like most places down this road, it attracts a fair percentage of the university rich-kids. I recommend coming here for breakfast, or during mid-afternoon when it's not heaving with Hooray Henries, and you'll have a chance to marvel at the stunning décor.

The Magic Café
110 Magdalen Rd
(01865) 794604
Open Mon-Sat 10am-6pm
Gourmet suppers each
Friday 7pm-10pm
Budget

This aptly-titled veggie café is a focal point for New Age Oxford, Pagan groups and those bizarre creatures known as the Cowley Road residents. A meeting place for the weird and wonderful, the food is fabulous and exactly what you'd expect, a tantalising range of interesting veggie dishes, herbal teas and mouth-watering cakes. The meals are usually less than a fiver and they even produce their own cookbook by Groovy Sue.

The time to really sample their food is Friday nights when the café stays open until 10pm and they cook exotic dishes with such names as 'Beneath the Smoky Mountain' and the 'Great Godzilla'.

The atmosphere is always relaxed and friendly (though beware early afternoons when it can get a little over-run with noisy kids), and on Saturday lunch times they even put on music events.

If that's not enough their free notice board is a cornucopia of everything from local witchcraft groups to Tai Chi lessons and Carnivores Anonymous.

Pizza Organic Restaurant
260 Banbury Road, Summertown
(01865) 554117
Open 11am-11pm Mon-Sun
Moderate

The bustling atmosphere here provides the perfect backdrop to enjoy pizza, grills (meat and fish) and pasta, washed down with wine, beer or soft drinks. Alternatively, try an organic veggie meal (there is a good choice), and if you are feeling a little naughty ask for some Hungarian ground paprika.

There are no downsides when eating here. Even the normal expense of eating organic does not show. So put your green hat on and join the merry throng.

INDIAN

Assam Balti
209 Cowley Road. (01865) 241493
Moderate

One of the many curry houses down the Cowley Road. It is small and intimate and has a good service with decent food, mid-range prices and is cheaper than Aziz, across the road.

The Aziz
228-230 Cowley Road
(01865) 794945
Open12pm-2.15pm & 6pm-11.15pm every day
www.aziz.uk.com
Moderate

One of Oxford's best Indians as much for its décor and friendliness as its food. You will be made to feel very special here and this, combined with their excellent curries, guarantees you'll be returning. When you become a real regular the manager will start to tell you about all the famous people that eat at The Aziz. It's a good idea to book as it gets busy most nights.

Chutneys
36 St Michaels Street
(01865) 724241 Open12am-2pm & 6pm-10.30pm
Moderate

Centrally located, bright and modern inside, its menu tells us

that it 'puts vegetarians first' and then lists a page of mainly meat starters! However, do come here for its food, as their dishes are very fresh and tasty. The drink and ice cream menu also complements the variety of main dishes. It is a bit annoying that the service is a little grumpy at times but you can partly put it down to the fact that they always seem so incredibly busy. Keep an eye out for the moving waterfall picture, which doesn't quite fit with the rest of the 90s interior. Remember it's the food you're here for and you'll have a marvellous time.

Kuri King
Cowley Road
Budget

Known locally as 'Kuri on Drinking'. Come here after the pubs have closed, buy a popadom or two and guzzle another ten pints to your heart's content. If you're coming here to eat, it's nothing exceptional but won't break the bank.

Shimla Pinks
16 Turl Street (01865) 244944
Open 12pm-2.30pm
& 6pm-11pm
6pm-10.30pm Sun
Expensive

Terence Conran meets India in the heart of Oxford. Modern, classy and friendly atmosphere with excellent Indian food.

Uddins Manzil
123 Walton Street
(01865) 556153 Open 12pm-2.30pm/6pm-12am
Budget

'The best chicken patia in Britain' Peter Huddleston, author of 'Tasty Birds'. This dark, 30-year-old curry house also offers plenty of veggies dishes.

LEBANESE

Al-Shami
25 Walton Crescent
(01865) 310066 12pm-12am Mon-Sun
Moderate

Being one of my favourite Oxford restaurants, I can safely recommend that to get the most variety and tastiness out of your Lebanese food make sure you mix and match the number of starters from the huge list which includes 23 veggie choices. There is also a tremendous selection of halal meat and the more adventurous among you may want to try the house speciality, lamb's brain salad. The atmosphere here is refreshingly chatty and lively and the waiters seem to be forever running around like headless chickens.

This is a great restaurant for eating with a large crowd of friends, as the last time I went there were 25 of us, and it was fantastic. For birthdays, they'll also make cakes if you ask.

Top tips:
Make sure you get an Al Shami credit card sized calendar. Very useful.

MODERN ENGLISH AND CONTINENTAL

The Cherwell Boathouse
Bardwell Road
(01865) 552746 12pm-2pm & 6pm-10pm Mon-Sun
www.cherwellboathouse.co.uk
Expensive

With its idyllic location by the river, The Boathouse is cosy, intimate, non-smoking, has no musak and does mouthwatering food. It has a very impressive global wine list, good veggie dishes, and when you book a table it's yours all night. During the summer months they put chairs and tables outside on the river's edge and if you come here during the day you can go punting before or after your meal. Make sure you book at least one week in advance during the summer though.

One last thing – it's a bit of a tricky place to find. If you're coming down Banbury Road out of Oxford centre keep your eyes peeled for roads to the right and you'll see Bardwell Road and a sign for the Boathouse. Follow your nose to the end of the lane.

Gee's Restaurant
61 Banbury Road (01865) 553540
Open Mon-Fri 12pm-2.30pm 6pm - 11pm Sun 12pm-12am
Expensive

Found a short way down Banbury Road, just before North Parade, this is one of Oxford's best-loved restaurants. Housed in an old-fashioned conservatory, which is packed with various plants, you will feel at first like you're entering a glorified tropical greenhouse, and half expect to see tiny chimpanzees swinging from the rafters.

The food is Mediterranean, with a variety of seafood, pasta dishes and steaks, many of which I've tried and found delicious. Gee's reputation for food is matched by its atmosphere, when, in the evenings, fairy lights serve to add to the magic of the place. Very friendly service.

The Lemon Tree
268 Woodstock Road
(01865) 311936 11am-11pm Sun 11am-10.30pm Parking
Expensive

Well-loved North Oxford restaurant and part of the Clinton Pugh dynasty of chic cafés and restaurants that stretch across the city. Sumptuous food, good wine and the best crème brûlée in town. This is a place where you feel it'd be rude not to indulge in a glass of port and a cigar at the end of a very satisfying meal. The restaurant has a pleasant 1920s colonial style and there's a warm atmosphere to the place. Definitely somewhere to be kept aside for special treats unless you're lucky enough to afford otherwise.

Quod Bar & Grill

92-94 High Street, Oxford
(01865) 202505 Breakfast served
8am-11.00am. Tea & coffee all day
Afternoon tea 3pm-6pm
Expensive

Big, chatty, spacious restaurant-cum-cocktail-bar that used to be a Barclays Bank. This is the kind of place where trendy, youngish business people take potential clients and students bring their parents (provided dad's paying). The big wall mounted paintings add a nice touch and make it feel like you're eating in Tate Modern or somewhere in Soho. The food is not outstanding for the price but pleasant enough with a selection of pasta, pizza and grill dishes and attentive service.

Tip – make sure you order seperate veg as it doesn't come with the main meal as you might expect.

CHINESE

The Rice Box

178 Cowley Road (01865) 202138
Open Sun-Sat 5pm-12am
Budget

Situated half-way up the Cowley Road, this place is perfect if you're in a hurry or it's late and you want some quality food rather than the predictable burgers and kebab. It smells great inside and the food doesn't usually take more than five minutes to arrive. It's always heaving Fridays and Saturdays so don't expect a seat but every other time it's usually OK, and there's always papers lying around if you want to eat on your own.

I have no explanation for this picture being here

The food is pretty good and there's a fair veggie option. Take note, this is not a place to come for a night out, but is instead a fast-food place for the more discerning.

The Oriental Condor

20 Park End Street.
(01865) 250988 12pm-11.30pm
www.oriental-condor.co.uk
Budget

Authentic and sparse in style with a massive selection of dishes including plenty of veggie and meat dishes. It's common to see Chinese people eating here which can be taken as a sign of good quality. Beware, however, the awful karaoke-style music!

THAI

Bangkok House

42a Hythe Bridge Road
(01865) 200705
Open 12pm-3pm & 5.30pm-11pm
Tue-Sat, Sun 5.30-11pm, closed
Monday. Park in car park at
bottom end of George St
Moderate

An all-round delight and one of Oxford's finest restaurants. Indulge in its airy décor, carved furniture, wonderfully tasty Thai food and its regal presentation. The attentive service is second to none and if you needed any further recommendation, Cliff Richard and Paul Weller have eaten here (though not together) and there are pictures to prove it. A perfect restaurant for impressing on a first date.

Tip – The starters are great and, in particular, the mushroom and galangal soup which may take you to the verge of orgasm. If you do, there are complimentary tissues in the bathroom.

Chiang Mai

130a High Street
(01865) 202233
12.30pm-3pm
& 6pm-11pm Mon-Sun
Expensive

One of the best restaurants in Oxford if you like Thai food. Chiang Mai is centrally located and set inside a beautiful Tudor building with a lively ambiance. Starters and main courses are both generous in portions and cooked with great attention.

Tricky to find, if you are looking down the High Street from Carfax keep an eye out for their sign and it's down a little alleyway on your right. Probably a good idea to book a table.

JAPANESE

Gashi Gashi

96 Cowley Road
(01865) 200789
Mon-Sun 12pm-3pm &
7pm-11pm except Tue 12pm-3pm
and Wed closed all day
Moderate

Tucked away discretely on the Cowley Road, this authentic Otoshi bar/restaurant owes much of its reputation to the manager Jonathan, who lived in Japan for many years before bringing his knowledge of Japanese food back to dear old Blighty. For newcomers (of which I was one) he will talk you through the traditions of Sushi and Japanese eating as well as showing you how to eat the food properly. There *is* a technique.

The Sushi repertoire, amongst many other choices (including veggie) is a great, tasty way to jump in at the deep end. A nice bit of raw eel never hurt anyone so make sure you come here and delve into the menu and try something a bit daring.

Give yourself plenty of time for an enjoyable night ahead and try not to get too carried away drinking their Japanese beer, tempting though it is.

With all food purchased from source and all Japanese ingredients imported, this is the real McCoy.

The Mongolian Wok Bar

67-69 George Street.
(01865) 792919
Mon-Fri 12pm-12am Sat & Sun 12pm-2.30pm & 6pm-11.30pm
Moderate

If you like cooking but none of the associated hassle then the Wok Bar is the perfect place for you. Simply choose your ingredients, sauce, meat (if you want it), put it into a bowl and then give it to someone else to cook.

The serve-yourself section contains bowls with all kinds of veggies and meats alongside chili, garlic, soy sauces. The art is to get the mix right and that's where the suggested menus, hanging down in front of you, come in very useful. Veggies can have their dishes cooked in foil so the meaty oils don't merge into your carrot stir-fry.

There is also karaoke every night, starting at about 10.30pm, apart from Sunday. The Mongolian style of low-pitched nasal humming is not essential but might win you an admiring audience if you attempt Bohemian Rhapsody.

FRENCH

Le Petit Blanc
**71-72 Walton Street
(01865) 510999 Open 12pm-11pm
Mon-Sat, Sun 12pm-10pm
Expensive**

Half-owned by Raymond Blanc and Richard Branson, this is a popular restaurant in the heart of Jericho with chic, convivial surroundings and excellent quality food. The menu changes weekly with a particularly fine selection of puddings and an extensive wine selection. Keep your eye out for the good value set menus, between 12pm and 3pm, if you want to try this food on a cheaper budget.

Friendly and accommodating to everyone from ankle-biters to B-list celebrities, watch out, however, for Richard Branson, he's notorious for scrounging taxi fares and never paying them back.

Café Noir
**3 Osler Road, Headington
(01865) 741300 Mon-Sat 10am-11pm, Sun 12pm-10.30pm kitchen shuts an hour before closing
Expensive**

Small French restaurant-bar with a calm, romantic atmosphere. It is

difficult to imagine you're in France with Oxford United around the corner but it's as close as you'll get in Oxford.

The service is laid-back and friendly and in the summer months you can sit at the pavement tables for that authentic Parisian feel. The food here is generally good and the monkfish comes highly recommended.

Bistro 20
**20 Magdalen Street
(01865) 246555 Mon-Sat 11am-5pm Sun 10am-4pm
Moderate**

Garish vault-bistro in central Oxford directly underneath the Randolph Hotel. Useful for pre-theatre stuff but not fantastic in décor or culinary delight. If you have only a smattering of taste you may enjoy the 'seen it before' menu and tacky Picasso-style etchings on the internal window in one of 1920s off-shoot rooms.

ITALIAN

Luna Caprese
4 North Parade
(01865) 554812
12pm-2pm & 6.30pm-11pm 7 days
Expensive

I was not particularly impressed with the food here and neither was my Italian girlfriend, who, unbeknown to the waiters, couldn't help overhearing them discuss their conquests at the local brothel. Not only that, the manager was argumentative over an issue with the bill that turned out to be his fault yet he didn't have the courtesy to apologise.

MEXICAN

Charly's Horse
61 St Aldates (01865) 242138
Cater for big parties Open 6pm-12am Tue-Fri, 5pm-12am Sat-Sun, (Kitchen closes at 10.30), closed Mondays
Expensive

With Hispanic rugs adorning the walls, Latino rhythms to tap your feet along to and the pungent smell of chilli, when you walk in to Charley's Horse you could almost be in the dizzy heights of Mexico City.

The food is quite expensive for what you get but very filling, with a good range of the Central American fajitas, enchiladas, nachos and guacamole. Great choice of margaritas too (if you get your receipt stamped enjoy a free margarita on your next visit) as well as other cocktails to choose from. Nice friendly service, comfy seats and until recently they did Salsa lessons here but the teacher is currently in Cuba doing national service. (A reasonable excuse).

Tip – go at the weekend for a better atmosphere.

Question – *Can anyone tell me the difference between a fajita, burrito and an enchilada?*

FISH

Fishers Restaurant
36/37 St Clement's Street
(01865) 243003 Open Mon-Sun 12pm-2.30pm & 6pm-10.30pm, Fri-Sat until 11pm and Sun 10pm
Expensive

Fantastic fish restaurant championed by several friends who rate it as their favourite Oxford eatery. The Zimbabwean chef has created a mixture of Mediterranean and Pacific Rim dishes and thus you can find yourself eating char-grilled shark or pan fried barracuda. If that doesn't tickle your fancy then try lobster (from Nova Scotia), salmon fishcakes or good old-fashioned fish and chips, although at nine quid this is not Harry Ramsden's.

Add to this a pleasant service, a nice chatty atmosphere and you have a recipe for success. Sitting near the large windows may mean you get passers-by gazing at your seconds but that's a small price to pay.

They used to have a goldfish in a bowl near the till but a number of customers complained about their unease at eating the little fish's friends, while it merrily swam around in endless circles, and so one day it mysteriously disappeared. Are you thinking what I'm thinking?

Thai restaurant at the Crazy Bear

PIZZAS

Mario Pizzeria Trattoria
103 Cowley Road
(01865) 722955
Eat In or Takeaway
Moderate

The food here is homely, basic and tasty and although not mind blowing, the fact that it always seems to be busy says something. If you are lucky you'll see Mario cruising the streets of Oxford on his Lambretta and if you're very lucky he'll show you his arse as he speeds past.

Pizza Organic Restaurant
(see organic restaurant section)

OUT OF OXFORD

Crazy Bear
Bear Lane Stadhampton
(01865) 890714
(Thai Restaurant) Open every day except Tuesdays
(English Restaurant) food from 12pm-3.00pm, 7pm-10.00pm
Sun 12pm-3.30pm
Expensive

This renowned hotel/restaurant on the outskirts of Oxford has in fact both Thai and English

Agoraphobics night at the Crazy Bear

restaurants on its premises, so when you've finished your tempura soup and red curry you can pop next door for treacle sponge pudding. Although I've only had a starter here the food looks delicious and the place has an excellent reputation.

Famous for having bowls of Japanese fighting fish on every table, you'll even find them in the toilet cistern, so please flush gently. Book in advance.

Somewhere Special

Rosamund the Fair

Found at the bottom of Jericho on the canal. Castlemill Boatyard Street
(01865) 553370 £50 a head
Expensive

Run by salty sea dog Tim Matthews for ten years now, this is probably Oxford's most romantic restaurant. For a sum that wouldn't break the bank (but might mean a couple of weeks in) you get a three-hour cruise through the canals and rivers of Oxford centre, with a choice of English and French cuisine freshly cooked on board.

Ideal for groups of twos and fours, the atmosphere is one of intimacy and romance as the boat only seats 24, and for the devilishly romantic men among you this is the ideal place to take the girlfriend to pop the big question. For the ladies, if you want to woo him into buying you a new dishwasher, the same applies.

Open Valentine's Day to the end of December. Closed Jan-Feb 13th, when it becomes a children's roller disco.

DELICATESSENS

Nellie's Deli

36 Great Clarendon Street
(01865) 557824
9am-7pm Mon-Sat
10.30am-6pm Sun

Tucked away down the back streets of Jericho, this old deli has been run now for 15 years by its Persian owner Mr Yazdan and sells a varied selection of wine and continental food. With everything from unusual herbs and spices to good Italian cakes and American ice cream, there should be something here for everyone's palate. My favourites thing he sells is Langues de Chat (cat's tongues). I have a habit of buying a box, eating them all in one go and then spending the rest of the day feeling ill.

Gluttons Deli

110 Walton Street
8.30am -7pm Mon-Fri 8.30am-6pm Sat 9.30am-5pm Sun

Good selection of Belgian beers, nice cookies, cakes, cheese and meats.

Taylors

31 St Giles (01865) 558853
8am-7.30pm Mon-Fri
8am-6pm Sat, 9am-6pm Sun

A well-loved delicatessen found on the corner of St Giles and Little Clarendon Street. It stocks ground coffee, fresh olives, cheese, enticing cakes and over-priced olive oil. They also have a sandwich bar for tasty lunchtime nibbles. Good place for celebrity spotting as Lloyd Grossman and Ronnie Barker both come here occasionally.

SPECIALIST FOOD SHOPS

Eastern Continental Stores

(Indian Supermarket)
Cowley Road, opposite Tescos

Lung Wah Chong

(Chinese Supermarket)
Hythe Bridge Road, 10am-7pm daily

Fasta Pasta

Covered Market (01865) 241973

Small Italian deli decorated with olives.

WHERE TO GET RIZLAS AT 4AM

B2

Corner of Headington Hill and Windmill Road
Open 24 hours a day, every day, including Christmas day

You need never have to smoke tea-bags wrapped in newspaper ever again but remember, some poor sod has to spend their Christmas in there just in case you forget to buy mince pies for the Queen's speech. What a depressing thought.

LATE-NIGHT EATING

Bodrum Kebabs

242 Cowley Road
(01865) 249981
Mon-Sat 11am-2am-ish (or as late as there's people around)
Sun 1pm-2am

The best veggie kebab in the world if sampled after a ten-hours drinking marathon down the Cowley Road, but then you'd probably feel the same about your shoes if they were lightly grilled and garnished with coriander.

Peppers

84 Walton Street
(01865) 310044 12pm-2.30pm & 5.30pm-11.30pm (12pm Fri and Sat)

Well-loved burger joint in Jericho with a good selection of sauces.

Kebab Vans

Price of a doner kebab varies from £2-£3

Found all over the city from the High Street all the way to St Giles and open till late especially at weekends. Particularly popular with University students, some of whom form strong allegiances with particular vans and will defend their honour to the death.

Nightlife

WATERING HOLES

What Oxford might lack in the way of nightclubs, it makes up for with its pubs. From the exotic stature of Freud's wine bar to the tiny tumble-down lop-sided cupboard that is The Bear, Oxford is a drinker's paradise. If you're looking for pubs with a bit of character or history, avoid George Street and you can't go too wrong. After all, many of these places have been the watering holes of famous writers, politicians and scholars for centuries. Walk into the White Horse and chances are everyone from Michael Palin to Tony Blair has at some time stood on the same spot as you and ordered a pint of beer and a packet of Cheesy Wotsits.

As JRR Tolkein once said –

'Inspiration comes in many forms but none lovelier than a pint of Speckled Badger.'

PUBS IN THE CITY CENTRE

The Bear
Alfred Street (01865) 721783

This is simply one of Oxford's most beautiful pubs, tucked away past the Oxford Museum, with its wooden interiors, low ceiling and outrageously uneven floors.

In summer everyone sits outside in the beer garden but to get the true spirit of the Bear you have to sit inside where after several pints you'll feel like you're inside a small wooden boat. This pub is famous for its underwhelming collection of ties which adorn the walls and ceiling, don't try and give them yours though as they still have several thousand lying around. In the 1950s, the landlord (a huge Harpo Marx fan) used to carry a car horn and scissors wherever he went, and at the end of the night after he'd had a few he would walk around blowing the horn deafeningly into the customers ears. Then, while they were still reeling from the shock he'd cut their ties off and stick them on the wall. And so the collection grew to what it is today, and includes ties of such distinguished celebrities as Les Dennis and Marilyn Manson.

Also worth mentioning is Eric's Tuesday evening quiz. Come and pit your wits against the professionals, as the University Challenge teams are often spotted down here practicing for the real thing. If you're left feeling stupid after coming last, make yourself feel better by challenging the weediest one to an arm wrestle.

The Eagle and Child
St Giles (01865) 310154
food 12am-2.30pm

This pub has lost a bit of its magic over the last couple of years with minor refurbishments, a fruit machine and intrusive bland music, but you'd have to work really hard to completely spoil its charm. Like its neighbour across the road, the Lamb and Flag, this pub has a deep literary history and has been famous as an academic haunt for many decades. Its

fame comes principally from The Inklings; a writers group who used to meet here every Thursday from the 30s to the 60s to discuss their work. The group consisted, amongst others, of Tolkein and CS Lewis and it is said that Tolkein saw the pub so much as his second home that he kept his slippers behind the bar. The room the writers all met in was called the Rabbit Room, (the area opposite the end of the bar) and it is said that after an all-day binging session on absinthe, Hugo Dyson, a member of the group, became convinced that tiny people with hairy feet were trying to steal his pipe. This event, of course, was to be the catalyst for Tolkein's masterpiece.

The clientele nowadays is a mix of Town and Gown and although it is no longer as hip as its neighbour, the pub still has some wonderful little cubby holes to slink away in and lose yourself in a good Narnia book. The most coveted spots are the wood panelled areas by the window on the way in. The bar-food is nothing exceptional and hearing Robbie Williams blaring out utterly kills the mystique of the place but a visit to Oxford without having a pint here would be less than complete.

Gloucester Arms

Friar's Entry (01865) 241177
Just behind the Oxford Playhouse

This self-proclaimed Rockers pub allows the punter to experience 'the best jukebox in the world' and DJs who play Gothic, Industrial and Blues on Tuesday night, Rock on Thursday and Hardcore Rock on Friday night. Furthermore, you can sing along with the live acoustic Blues on Sundays.

The low lighting and Rockers ambience sits strangely alongside the wall mounted photos of Victor Spinetti, Canon and Ball and the marvellous Bucks Fizz. There is a simple answer. This pub has the closest proximity to a theatre stage door (The Playhouse) in Britain. We measured the gap and it came to three feet. 'Tetley Steve' will tell you all about the actors they've had in, including Nicholas Lyndhurst's flying stories and the wild drinking antics of Basil Brush. Mark, the landlord, will also fill you in on bikers clubs and Rock information. If you like Rock, actors, jukeboxes, acoustic music and a nice pint, this is the place for you. If you like bland theme pubs with no atmosphere, go in the pub next door.

The King's Arms

40 Hollwell Street (01865) 242369

This large white pub sits on the corner of Parks Road and Hollywell Street slap-bang in the middle of town and is always very busy and popular. The place has a few interesting nooks and crannies, especially at the back, and is adorned with hundreds of photographs of punters, past and present, including a picture of the Queen Mum downing a pint of snakebite.

Not only is the pub usually teeming with students, but you'll also find a high propensity of dandruff-riddled lecturers dotted around the place. These poor creatures, cocooned by the academic lifestyle, generally congregate in twos or threes and are best left alone to skulk in the corners babbling away in their own bewildering manner about convoluted theories and the price of corduroy. If you need a seat and there's nowhere to sit, show them a picture of a woman and it should be enough to frighten them away and earn you a comfy seat. The pub also sells real ale, has a non-smoking room and sells very average bar food. I've always found the place somewhat smug (in a Jeremy Paxman sort of way) and compared to the other pubs in its close vicinity it lacks a certain charm.

Men, look out for the graffiti in the Gents toilets –

'Talbot Poncenby has an arse like a wind sock'.

The Lamb and Flag
St Giles (01865) 515787

Originally an old coach house, this is now one of Oxford's best-loved pubs. Even from the outside, with its narrow passageway, etched frosted windows and pastoral design, it seems a conspiratorially inviting pub. Once the haunt of some of Oxford's esteemed writers; Grahame Greene wrote about it and Hardy weaved it into Jude the Obscure. In fact, the whole place has an academic dreaminess to it, especially the front part, with its wood panelling, coats of arms and low iron chandelier, giving the feeling that you could almost be sat in some old Victorian study.

The back end of the pub has lots of fabulous little cubby holes for canoodling, conspiring or just losing yourself in. There's one in particular by the bar, which must have once been a cupboard but is now a tiny one-man open cell for the penance of the solitary drinker or a chance to catch up with some studying whilst enjoying the atmosphere.

The place is almost exclusively a student bar, but this shouldn't make you feel like an outsider, on the contrary, it's very welcoming. The best time to come is early evening (before the masses pack it out) and find a table where you can linger over a drink or two with a good novel or a notebook full of ideas and good intentions. The old fire at the back is never lit, more's the pity, and the place smells gently of hamster cages, and old woodlands.

The pub toilet is the only one I've ever visited that sells resolve, anadin and bisodol. This is a place that knows some serious drinking is going to take place every night.

The Old Tom
101 St Aldates (01865) 243034

This is an odd sort of place that looks like it could almost have been lifted from the East End and despite being sandwiched down St Aldates between two universities, The Old Tom attracts as many bus-drivers as it does students.

The bit by the bar just on your way in, known as Compost Corner, seems permanently occupied by a group of locals having a moan about the traffic schemes and who look like the kind of people who do taxidermy for a hobby. The rest of the pub is usually full of Pembroke and Christ Church students struggling over the Daily Express crossword. Don't get excited about the food, it's predictably bland pub grub but what this place lacks in culinary expertise it makes up for with a great beer garden at the back.

The Royal Oak
Woodstock Road (01865) 248011

Large student pub, a short walk down the beautiful Banbury Road. Making good use of the space inside, this place has all the best bar games including pool, bar billiards and table football, yet is still perfect for slinking off into a corner and having a good gossip. Get there early to bag the sofa by the pool table otherwise you'll find the likes of St Anne's divas Sarah and Emily hanging out there. There's plenty of seating outdoors for a cool Pimms on a hot summer's evening and the only bad thing I could say about the place is, like so many other Oxford pubs, if you like your bar food pricey and unadventurous look no further.

Three Goats Heads
St Michael's Place (01865) 721523

While the upstairs room is decorated with frighteningly dull architectural maps, the downstairs bit looks like a

swimming pool mixed with a gents urinal. That aside, this is an unpretentious, relaxed pub with cheap strong lager on tap, and a cellar bar for finishing your essay on a quiet afternoon.

The clientele are a mixed bag of students and locals and despite being popular the place never gets uncomfortably busy like so many of the other student haunts in the town centre. The food is, dare I say it, well above the quagmire of blandness that most pubs dish out here, and to top it all I met some really friendly people last time I was here.

The Turf Tavern
4 Bath Place (01865) 243235

One of Oxford's best-known and most cherished pubs, the Turf has for years maintained that delicate balance of being a huge hit with visitors and tourists whilst maintaining its character, host of regulars and popularity with students.

The secret location of the pub is part of its charm, for to reach the Turf you have to go down a gloomy alleyway (once known as Hell passage), and just as you start to think some 19th century street urchin is going to leap out and relieve you of your handbag, you find yourself in a courtyard full of noise, laughter and the enticing smell of pub grub.

The Turf is relatively small inside (though extremely cozy in winter) whereas outside it has three large seating areas, all of which seem full most times of the day in summer.

The beers are reputed to be the best in Oxford, with an endless stream of new ones on tap every week to keep you on your toes, including their wonderful green beer (which is exactly how it sounds).

If you only had an afternoon to visit Oxford, forget trawling around colleges and museums, spend it here instead, lolling around and experimenting with the beers. This is where the heart of the city is.

The Wheatsheaf
129 High Street (01865)243276

Tucked down an alleyway off the High Street, this is a tasteful and popular haunt with the sporty student crowd as well as being home to Jazz Club 'Spin' on a Thursday. While the bar-food is woefully mundane and the décor somewhat predictably focused on Oxford's academic history, it's still a place where you can see hoards of ruddy cheeked young men in tweed and enjoy a pint of Hoegaarden, if that's your turn on.

It also has, rather surprisingly, a book exchange system, presumably for travellers, so when you've finished The Beach you can swap it for something else, although they usually only have about five to choose from so don't get too excited. The more adventurous among you might like to try and find regular punter Giles and ask him about the story of Wilbur his teddy bear if you want a good laugh.

Spin at the Wheatsheaf
Thursday 8.30pm £4
Popular upstairs venue showcasing Jazz, Blues and funky bands.

Tuesdays there's a student Jazz jam, which, if you're in town with your Souzaphone and fancy doing a spot of Miles Davis, might be up your street.

The White Horse
52 Broad Street (01865) 721860

Squashed down Broad Street and surrounded by colleges and Blackwell's Bookshops, the pub attracts a marvellous wealth of characters, from the sozzled staff of local bookshops to scary looking tramps who normally turn out to be dysfunctional college lecturers.

Look for the Trinity College croquet club photo in the right-hand corner of the pub; the bloke in the middle looks like he is wearing huge shoes. If you can't find it, ask Andy the barman or regular Mike and they'll put you right. In fact both are a wealth of stories about the pub and its eccentric customers, from Arselips (an old regular with a little white beard whose mouth looks like a quivering cat's rectum) to Camel man and Captain Birdseye.

One old guy is the now-retired old Welsh porter for the Bodleian Library, who on more than one occasion, half-way through his drink would suddenly exclaim 'Oh Shit,' and dash out of the pub after realising he'd forgotten to lock up the library again.

The pub does some of the best beer in Oxford and despite its diminutive size, is well worth the effort to visit, just pray that the party of six students by the window will bugger off soon and give up their seats.

Best time to visit is late October when they are host to Oxford's annual conker championship.

PUBS ON THE COWLEY ROAD, IFFLEY ROAD & ST CLEMENT'S

Bar Baby
Cowley Road
(01865) 202506

As an antidote to the rough-and-ready pubs in the Cowley area, this place first marked the appearance of the trendy bars in Oxford. Overlooking the equally stylish Penguin fish bar, Bar Baby is in essence a London-feel designer bar, with a few nice features but very little in the way of genuine character. Attracting a young, posy crowd it boasts some plush brown leather chairs and cool lighting effects, but lets itself down with predictably dull, pumping dance music and a distinct lack of seating. If you're under 21 and fed up with crappy locals you'll love it. If you've ever lived in London or Brighton, you'll probably avoid it. If you're over ten and a half stone, you probably won't be let in.

Baba
Cowley Road

If Habitat and Muji got together to design a bar, this would be it. From the moment you walk through their gorgeous American diner-style doors, you enter a stylish, minimalist palace. Decorated in chrome and copper, with huge mirrors and sprawling leather seating, the atmosphere is intimate, relaxed, and conducive to a good natter. Attracting a slightly older, more discerning crowd than its competitor Bar Baby, this place really is worth the trek up the Cowley Road.

The joys of class A drugs

The Elm Tree
95 Cowley Road (01865) 244706

Spit and sawdust pub up the Cowley Road with a comfortable mix of students and Irish locals. The décor is pretty awful but the place gets top marks for atmosphere. Run by the old landlord from the Bully, this is the kind of pub where, if you felt like getting completely hammered you'd enjoy it the best.

Look out for the bizarre dog-porn photo next to the bar, and try not to trip over the portly sausage dog that's always wandering around. They also do Irish folk sessions on Wednesday and Sunday and have local bands in the room next door from Thursday to Saturday. All things considered, pubs don't come much better than this.

The Half Moon
17 St Clement's St (01865) 247808

Once Oxford's smallest pub, now a simple, quiet Irish local, dotted with the odd student and an array of colourful old regulars. The side of the bar by the fire feels like someone's living room, in fact last time I was in here, all the old guys were crowded round the telly watching 'Who Wants to Be a Millionaire?' which somehow made me feel like I was in the film 'Waking Ned'.

Local characters include 'Mr Bull', a 70-year-old Irish gent who, if you buy him a pint, will tell you stories about the pub and declare *'all my lies are true.'* Another to look out for is Black Tom. Legend has it he was once found with his trousers down by his ankles, a cigar up his arse and his shit in the urinal. This is a real drinkers pub.

The New Inn
119 Cowley Road (01865) 247519

Something of a legend in these parts, the New Inn has doggedly stuck to the same image, clientele and sanitary hygiene in the ten years that I've been here.

Attracting a miasma of die-hard Goths, Punks, floppy-fringed Indie kids and subversive looking weirdos on the verge of a nervous breakdown, this is the haven for Oxford's grubby muso crowd, as the memorabilia and posters on the ceiling prove. Its décor leaves a lot to be desired, from the toilet seat above the bar, to its god-awful carpet and the hideously tacky spider's web on the ceiling (although the tack is part of its charm). The

A cheeky tale

It was after an evening drinking in the New Inn that I gatecrashed a party over the road with a friend. After an 'incident' involving the odd breakage or three, things turned nasty and the cops were called. The two of us ended up escaping by getting onto the roof and scrambling over the Cowley rooftops assisted by a guy with a leg in full plaster cast, who was already up there on the roof! We never found out who he was or what he was doing up there in the first place, but I'd like to take this opportunity to thank him for saving our skins. I wonder if he's still up there?

poster advertising Amazulu and the Q-Tips must has been up for the last eight years at least.

This is however, one of those rare gems – a pub of eccentric characters and wild stories. If you want to find out the gossip on the local legends, this is the place to come. From The Jennifers to Death by Crimpers, there's a tale about every band and every musician in them. Come here regularly and you might be lucky enough to spot the odd familiar face.

If the guys from Trainspotting came to Oxford they'd drink here.

The Olde Ale House
Iffley Road

The sign outside claims 'unspoiled by progress' which seems to contradict the facelift it had last June when it used to be the Fir Tree. After much debate on how to describe the interior of the pub someone suggested *'designer higgledy-piggledy'*, which will have to make do for now. Despite the designer look, it has a welcoming atmosphere and seems the ideal place for a good pint of beer and a cosy chat.

The pub has an interesting layout and is littered with junk from bikes and records to old tin adverts on the walls and even an upside down record player on the ceiling like the one I had as a kid on which I played Tubby the Tuba.

Food is served until 9pm every night and they usually have about eight or nine beers on tap.

This pub is also rumoured to be where some of the more naïve male students learn all they need to know about sex from the 'Oh Wicked Wanda' book on the shelf, in the back room. So if you're still a little confused about the birds and the bees, come on your own, buy a lovely pint of bitter, turn to page 46 and start reading...

'Wanda smiled, and rolled over to present her dimpled derriere to the nymphet's ministrations......'

The Star
21 Rectory Road (01865) 248011

Decorated with Scooby Doo and cult movie posters you'd get no prizes for guessing that this is a popular student pub. Tucked away just off the Cowley Road and decorated outside with Christmas tree lights, the Star plays good music and has a friendly laid-back atmosphere. Its young, vaguely hip crowd are the sort of people who wear denim jackets and roll their own (a bit like the clientele from the New Inn but ten years younger), although women can be a bit thin on the ground here sometimes. At the back they've got a poolroom with a couple of tables and beyond that the big beer garden makes this a popular summer haunt, even if it is a bit shabby. Watch out at last orders, they stick on these dazzling halogen lights and when everyone sees exactly whom they've been chatting up they usually beat a hasty retreat.

All in all, however, this is a well-loved pub and deservedly so.

The Temple Bar
21 Temple Road Cowley
(01865) 243251

Undoubtably one of Oxford's coolest pubs. Over the years this place has grown from strength to strength, attracting a crowd who'd be more likely to have Pavement in their record collection than Marillion. The back end of the pub is sort of American diner style with two pool tables, table football and cheap school dinner-hall tables which only the Temple Bar could pull off as being almost stylish. At weekends it gets very busy and can get devilishly smoky too but you can always tumble out into their beer-garden-come-car-park.

Favourite haunt of some of the local pop alumni as well as pretty much all the people I know and love in this town.

PUBS IN JERICHO

Harcourt Arms
1 Cranham Terrace (01865) 310360

With two open fires and a collection of board games at the bar, this pub does have an incredibly homely feel to it despite the fact that the landlord looks like a mad scientist. With subtle lighting and no thumping music it makes a fantastic Jericho local. The clientele seem to be a mixed bag of graduates and thirty-somethings, not the sort of people who start singing Roll out the Barrel after half ten, more the kind of people who love a good debate. Bar snacks are served until 10pm weekdays and 9pm weekends.

Jude the Obscure
54 Walton Street (01865) 553344

Despite being named after one of the most depressing novels in the English language this is among my favourite pubs in Oxford. Seeming to effortlessly attract a mix of Town and Gown it is one of those rare places that from the moment you enter you feel like you're visiting an old friend.

Plenty of the pub's charm has been supplied by landlord Noel Reilly, a thin, chain-smoking Irish intellectual who arrived in 1995 when it was the notoriously rough Prince of Wales. After Noel took over he cleared most of the old crowd out by running a policy of 'no swearing and no drinking out of bottles', followed by playing Radio 3 and 4 all day, every day, until the rest finally buggered off.

Nowadays it is painted *'the same green as used in mental hospitals to calm the patients'*, is filled with colourful paintings, and even has theatre lights in the left bar for the occasional play. And Noel's

Inside Freud's wine bar

propensity for a good natter also seems to have rubbed off on the place. This is, after all, the man who at his last pub in Swindon, brought in a Czechoslovakian philosopher to lecture his customers.

It's a brilliant pub any day of the week and in summer you can let your conversations spill out into the beer garden.

COCKTAILS AND AFTER HOURS DRINKING

Freud

119 Walton Street (01865) 311171

Effortlessly converted from a church to a cocktail bar years ago, Freud's is simply one of the most beautiful places to eat and drink in Oxford. As soon as you enter it's impossible not to be impressed by the character of the place from its stain-glassed windows, variety of different art-work that usually adorns the walls and its sheer size. Of course you could be forgiven for thinking that parts of the

place are incredibly run-down but I think this designer grottiness is a feature chosen by its idiosyncratic owner (although I've heard him described in less favourable terms).

The drinks are unsurprisingly expensive but the cocktails are wonderful, try the Mexican Lullaby for starters, plus you can watch the bar-staff showing off after months of watching the Tom Cruise film 'Cocktail' in slow motion. There's a good range of customers in here but predictably a fair share of posh students. You might hear horsy laughs from the ladies and some of the men believe themselves to be god's gift to womankind but don't let them put you off coming, you can have a sophisticated evening even if you are surrounded by riff-raff.

For any lovers of the ancient game of 'Go', Oxford Go Society meet here Tuesdays and Thursdays, around 6.30pm and you can sit down and have a game or two with them.

They're a bit nerdy but harmless enough.

Weekends can get outrageously busy so if you want to avoid the crowds this place is ideal as an early start to the evening with a cool cocktail or Horlicks if you're driving.

Raouls Cocktail Bar
32 Walton Street (01865) 553732

This place seems to attract too much of a yuppie crowd for my liking but is definitely worth investing a little time in if cocktails are your tipple. They have a fair selection for between three and four quid and 'Mutiny on the Bounty' comes highly recommended.

Beware at weekends, it can get horribly busy and claustrophobic. Raoul's is best visited during the week when you can marvel at their odd mix of ethnic art, cubist prints and artexed walls downstairs. Not sure about the in-house DJ though, he always seems to be playing boring dance music. Given the look of the place I'd give it a really wild Jazz soundtrack from the likes of Art Blakey or Alice Coltrane.

Duke of Cambridge
Little Clarendon St (01865) 558173
Happy hour 5.30pm-7pm

A cocktail and wine bar kind of place with London prices. Loud, bustling and popular with students it is, however, situated on Little Clarendon Street so don't be surprised if the jolly hockey sticks crowd is here in force. Weekends can get outrageously busy and a bit abrasive so if you want to claim a large seating area get there early.

AFTER-HOURS DRINKING HOLES

The Brickworks
Cowley Road

Once Rats, a rugger-buggers hangout, this place is now a charming no-frills late-night drinking bar. Open until 12am at weekends, there's no charge, but you might have to eat a plate of chips to keep them happy.

It's a good place to come for your final bout of drinking if you're in the area, especially as the booze is cheap, but I don't really know what to make of the place at all. It looks like the sort of bar you might stumble across in a hostel in Amsterdam. The fake brick style is wonderfully bad, there's no heating, the girl behind the bar talks for England and I can't make the clientele out at all. And the sign in the temporary gent's toilet – 'Sorry it's only temporary' has been up for years.

There are also several eating places along the Cowley Road that serve as convenient after-hours drinking establishments for the boozedup desperados. Ask around and you'll find out who they are.

OFF THE BEATEN TRACK

The Trout
195 Godstow Road Lower Wolvercote
(01865) 302071

To get here follow the Woodstock road all the way to the ring-road then take a left into Wolvercote and you'll find the Trout.

Boasting its fair share of idiosyncracies, across the river on the opposite bank is a strange garden with stone lions and other odd things in it, while over the river itself hangs a dilapidated wooden bridge straight out of Tomb Raider. The pub also has two resident peacocks, Darren and Shirley, who will happily share your dinner with you, especially if you're having the pub's speciality birdseed salad.

The mixture of beautiful surroundings and excellent food means that in summer The Trout is usually packed with tourists, while during term time it seems a popular place for students to bring mum and dad. In fact the pub always seems busy, try coming mid-afternoon in February and you'll see.

As a consequence it has become somewhat the victim of its own success and despite its size can still be hard to get a seat, while queues for the food can be tiresome, so make

The beer garden at the Perch

sure you arrive very early lunchtime or evening. But if you can handle the crowds, The Trout is a near-idyllic country pub, which on a warm summer's afternoon is a rare treat.

The Perch
Bisney Lane off the Botley Road
(01865) 240386 Does Food

The younger brother of the Trout, inside it's too much fake 'olde worlde' for my liking with stuffed fish, horse brass and whatnot but it doesn't matter too much because you'll want to sit outside anyway. To reach it go up the Botley Road past the station, look for signs to the golf course then follow the track for ages until you find the pub at the end. During winter it's fairly unspectacular but in summer it's packed with tourists.

(See parks and gardens section for how to walk to the Perch and the Trout from Port Meadow)

The Black Boy

91 Old High Street, Headington Village
(01865) 763234

Worth popping in if you happen to be in the area, but forget the main bar and head straight for the wonderfully titled Snug Bar at the back of the pub. Full of 'old farts' (as the barmaid put it) this is one of those classic old style bar-rooms with dented brass-look tables and an array of jumble cluttering the shelves around the room. Look out for the woodpecker and Guiness clock, which would probably sell for thousands at a car boot sale. Your visit won't be rewarded by this alone, but combine it with the pub's good selection of beers and you're half way there.

Make sure you acquaint yourself with Landlord Robert Moore, he is a local legend, not only for being the person in Oxford to get racing tips off, but also because he performs with his own band 'Jonny Snatch and the Beef Curtains'.

A drinking tale

About 8 years ago, I was sitting in the Black Boy, in the Snug Bar with a few friends, and at our table was sat this frail old gentleman guy, knocking back pints of Guiness as if the world were about to end. After a while we struck up a conversation and he introduced himself as 'Spaz' and said he was an old drinking partner of Dylan Thomas. I took him at first to be a trifle deluded but he started to pull all these bits of paper out of his wallet and show them to me. They were a crumbling collection of photos of himself and the drunken Welshman, along with a handful of poems, one or two of which were dedicated to him. He spoke fondly of their time together and Dylan's passion for alcohol, and I asked him what he was doing in Oxford. He explained he was washed out, lonely and waiting to die, his only comfort was the booze. Then he turned to me and a twinkle returned to his eyes, and he said —

'Forty years ago Dylan and I decided to have a drinking competition. First one to drink themselves to the death was the winner.' Course Dylan won, and I've been trying to catch up with him ever since…'

Beware of football days, the pub gets very busy. Beware even more of the Oxford football team who occasionally drink here, they have a reputation for being, shall we say, a little egotistical. So if a guy with a mullet haircut and bum-fluff moustache asks you if you want to shake his hand, you'll know why.

The Isis Tavern
Iffley Lock, Iffley village

Only accessible to the public by foot from Donnington Bridge or the lock, (via Iffley village), and with an expansive garden overlooking the river, this place has always had the potential of being one of Oxford's most stunning pubs. Hard times, however, turned it into a ghastly theme pub last year, and it now is nothing better than a family chain pub with an overbearing and largely irrelevant nautical theme and crap food.

I probably wouldn't be quite so damning if it hadn't been my local for a year, but it always breaks my heart to see another good pub ruined. Fishing paraphernalia and gripes aside, the location is fantastic, and it's perfect if you're ambling down the lock one summer's afternoon and fancy a little refreshment.

Tradition decrees that the architecture students from Brookes University have their results pinned up on the tree every year, in the garden.

UNIVERSITY BARS

Most University bars are a sorry state of affair, and with so many wonderful pubs in Oxford you'd be chomping at the bit after spending the night in one of these dingy caverns. Saying that, there are a few exceptions, notably New College, Wadham and Magdalen. Wadham is great in summer as the bar spills out onto the lawns, Magdalen is very beautiful and has a riverside terrace while New College is proud of its Wurlitzer juke-box. If you're not a University member you're more likely to be able to sneak in on weekdays as most weekends there'll be some sort of ticket policy or a bouncer, who, if he doesn't like the look of you, will require you to quote from The Iliad to get past him.

DISCOTHEQUES

Considering the enormous student population at the University and Brookes, combined with the locals and all the tourists that visit this town, the club scene in Oxford has always been something of an embarrassment. With many of the clubs here still erring more towards the Grange Hill school disco than the Big Beat Boutique, you might think you'd be better off staying at home with a copy of Ibiza anthems '92 and drinking Kestrel lager.

In the last few years however, with the refurbishments at the Bully and Zodiac down the Cowley Road, and places like Po Na Na and Yesbut opening up in town, people in Oxford have finally begun to realise there is more to clubbing than waving your arms around to 'Hi Ho Silver Lightning'. And in fact events like Strange Fruit at YesBut and Thursday's special guest DJ slot at Po Na Na prove that the demand is there for excellent cutting edge music nights.

So whatever your taste (if you have any), Oxford's meagre collection of clubs should be able to tempt out even the most eclectic audiophiles for a night of fun. And if you're looking for 80s disco, mirrored ceilings and somewhere to swing your handbag, welcome to heaven.

Soon to have his own show on Channel Four

The Bullingdon Arms
Cowley Road (01865) 244516

Back in the dark ages the Bully was a fabulous spit and sawdust Irish pub with a room at the back that was essentially a rubbish tip with old tyres, crates and a broken down van, but it didn't stop the landlord using it as a beer garden. Those days are long gone and now the back room is a function room host to a variety of gigs and club nights.

Fridays for a while now have been home to Retro, a mix of 70s and Michael Jackson that somehow warps into House and Garage by the end of the night. The DJs are unintentionally hilarious Ali G types parading around on the stage with microphones forever shouting -

'Yes, yes, Oxford's finest in the house,' and other gibberish. Look out also for the tall guy who looks a bit like Brett Anderson from Suede and stands motionless on the dance floor with his hand in the air looking like he's directing traffic. What's that all about?

Saturdays vary from special gigs to Trance/Dance nights while Thursday are usually reserved for local Indie gigs and occasional Jazz and Easy Listening. Even Paul Young played here last year. Oh, how the mighty have fallen.

Don't get your hopes up too much about the venue itself, it is literally the back room of a pub but it's the friendly loved-up crowd who come here who will make you feel at home. And most importantly it's been blessed with that Cowley Road magic.

Club Latino
St Clement's (01865) 247214
£3-£5 entrance fee depending on the day of the week

Akin to the first two circles of Dante's inferno, Club Latino is where foreign students and sleazy men are sent to pay penance for their fashion mistakes. The top circle is cold and lifeless with nowhere to sit, except in the TV room which always seems to be showing some Spanish soap opera.

As you descend into the second level of hell, your ears will pick up the torturous sound of Salsa-Europop. Down here, slip-on shoes and moustaches are derigueur (for men and women) and again there's nowhere to sit except a tiny booth in the corner by the bar that somehow feels like you're sat in a urinal.

Oxford's answer to a caravan site night-club without the Status Quo cover band.

Downtown Manhattan
George Street (01865) 721101

Applying the principle that if you wait long enough, you'll eventually come back into fashion, DTM has stuck determinedly to its neon tat, chart music and scrawny dance floor for over 20 years now. It's basically a dark, grubby club for the less discerning, with an awful monographed carpet and aerobics-class style mirrors on the dance floor where you can see your bald patch from 43 different angles. But as the dance floor is ridiculously small and the couple next to you will be practising their Dirty Dancing routine and slobbering in each other's ears, its best avoided anyway. The clientele are a strange bunch, ranging from virgin clubbers, lager boys and older women on the pull, to Tarquin and chums, in their chunky jumpers, on the look out for 'totty'.

Of all the nightclubs in Oxford, this is one of them.

Fifth Avenue
35 Westgate Centre (01865) 245136

Glamorously located inside a shopping centre and having acquired the nickname 'Filth Avenue', this is another Oxford meat-market stuck in the days when John Taylor's haircut was considered cool. Need I go on?

Park End
Park End Street (01865) 250181

Oxford's largest club, attracting the type of punters for whom size is everything. With three big dance floors and a huge capacity it does, however, attract the occasional big-name DJ and the likes of Ministry of Sound. And a recent £1 million make-over means the club has now got better air-conditioning, six bars, a new dance-floor and new décor.

All that aside, it's still horribly tacky and the mid-week student nights are probably the best times to come if you really have to. At weekends here

the different floors play everything from House anthems to Soul and R'n'B and the club is usually packed. Its popularity means you will invariably be queuing outside for a while which is a golden opportunity to get into an argument with some bloke who took offence to the way you were looking at his girlfriend, even though your back was turned to her.

Student nights are Monday for Brookes and Wednesdays for the University.

Po Na Na Souk Bar
13-15 Magdalen Street. (01865)249171
Open 9pm-2am

With a Moroccan touch to its décor, Po Na Na (named after the wombat in the Lion King) has a cool dance floor and two bars serving bottled beer and cocktails. A hip Town and Gown crowd happily mix in the various nooks and crannies, while others just seem to come here to get some kip in the bed just by the dance floor. Waiting for drinks is never too much of a problem but you could be queuing outside for a while, especially at weekends, if you arrive after pub closing. There also seems to be a fairly strict door policy that doesn't like big groups of lads so if there's a bunch of you it's best to turn up in twos and threes.

The music varies throughout the week with live Jazz-Funk beats on Wednesdays, while Thursdays offer some pretty awesome guest DJs from the likes of Portishead to Groove Armada. On Fridays and Saturdays the tunes are spun by DJ Tea, who has an eclectic assortment of Latin, Breakbeat, Soul and Deep Darjeeling. Probably the best club in central Oxford.

YesBut
George Street (01865) 726036

Small but cosy underground club done out in a sort of Mediterranean style. Unfortunately it's located in one of Oxford's less salubrious streets, which means it does tend to attract a lot of riffraff, some of whom haven't even got degrees. If busy it can feel a little claustrophobic, and the dance floor will only accommodate a few dozen before you start getting elbows in your face when 'Disco 2000' comes on and everyone starts to 'Jarvis'.

But this aside, it is definitely one of Oxford's better clubs, making an effort to put on some cool evenings, ranging from Acid Jazz nights to Hiphop and R&B. The one to especially look out for is Wednesday nights Strange Fruit. Expect a whole range of eclectic underground sounds as seven or eight DJs take it in turn, keeping you guessing what'll be next. Expect anything from Death in Vegas and DJ Shadow, to Belle and Sebastian or even Cliff Richard doing a cover of Ghostrider.

And I almost forgot, Wednesdays are free.

The Zodiac
Cowley Road (01865) 420042

Starting life as The Co-op Hall this was a venue where, back in the bad old days, you'd have to slip down a shabby alleyway, then up some stairs into what looked like your old school hall to see bands struggle through a crap PA. Nowadays the corridor has gone, the PA is top notch, it's a bit cleaner, but the school hall remains, host to innumerable bands every Saturday, and different club nights throughout the week.

As a venue the Zodiac is pretty good, being more intimate and cheaper than most London venues and often attracting plenty of big name bands for warm up gigs before their major tour. Be ready for a long wait at the bar however, it was renovated last year and made smaller for reasons which defy logic and now means that at busy gigs you could be waiting an awful long time for your vodka red bull.

Downstairs the cocktail bar is worth visiting as it usually plays different styles of music to whatever's going on upstairs, and tucked away in the corner Tom's bar has been given a sort of Gaudí look. More importantly this is somewhere you can escape the music, sit down and let Tom squeeze orange juice onto your forehead.

The club nights vary from Indie to Hard House. Wednesdays are renowned as being a shag-fest for students. They all pile in, get a drink from the bar then everyone starts grabbing. It's like musical chairs except the one left at the end is the loser. Described by FHM as the 'easiest shag in the country'.

The Saturday Indie night on the other hand is a cornucopia of pasty-faced kids in denim jackets. The music is more Indie greatest hits than cutting edge and the DJ plays everything from the mighty Pixies to the banal shite of Candy Flip.

Unlike most other clubs in Oxford, the Zodiac mercifully doesn't appeal to the usual town crowd who like nothing better than wearing swim-wear in sub-zero temperatures and a good fight. Instead, with its mix of students and Cowley Road regulars, the club is friendly, flirty and one of the best nights out you could have in Oxford.

And finally, while you're reaching for your disco clobber, a bit of good old fashioned parental advice –

if you hand your coat in at the cloakroom try everything in your power to leave ten minutes before the end, you'll save an awful long wait getting it after 2am, as the service is appallingly slow. And if you lose your ticket as I did last time I was there, then god help you, the kebab vans will be long gone before you get out.

SHAKESPEARE IN THE PARK

THEATRES

Apollo Theatre
George Street (01865) 244544

This 1930s theatre, designed with the rather surreal theme of Tutankhamun crossed with Italian street theatre, plays host to the typical big budget stuff with everything from West End musicals to boy bands, 60s revival bands and big-name comedians. Even wrestling has been on the menu recently.

No theatre is complete without its ghosts and The Apollo is no exception. Its three resident ghosts Helen, Jim and Jack were exorcised last year by visiting psychic Derek Acorah through a complicated ritual of mumbling, going red in the face and waving his hands about, although Jim refused to budge. Legend has it that his cold presence can still be felt in the top circle sometimes.

The Burton-Taylor Theatre
Gloucester Street (01865) 798600

Seasonal student-run theatre which puts on a chunky selection of contemporary drama, comedy and new writing from students and the local community. This is modern theatre at its most intimate and best.

The Old Fire Station
George Street (01865) 794494

180 capacity theatre with a predictable selection of mainstream theatre from Shakespeare to Pinter. Sort of the baby brother of the Apollo. The downstairs room is a café-bar by day, night-club by night. Look for the legs hanging down in the café bar then run away.

Pegasus Theatre
Magdalen Street (01865) 722851
www.pegasust.dircon.co.uk

Starting life as a converted school canteen 30 years ago, the Pegasus is now a centre for youth arts, contemporary dance, music, mime and underground theatre. The shows are usually a mix of locally-based youth productions and more underground professional touring companies. During the week they run youth workshops where potential luvvies can learn lighting, sound or stage management skills. If this interests you give them a ring on the number above, failing that I happen to know that they can be bribed with chuppa chups lollies. Worth supporting in a town where traditional theatre is too much a rule of thumb.

Legend has it that on Halloween at the stroke of midnight, the ghosts of the old dinner ladies can be seen wandering around smelling of boiled cabbage and soya mince. To free them from their nocturnal wanderings, a virgin student has to kiss their stubbly chins, then finish off second helpings of mashed potato.

hello

The Oxford Playhouse
Beaumont Street (01865) 798000

Usually this is the kind of place you'll see Prunella Scales doing Chekov or Judie Dench doing Pinter but they also put on everything from poetry slams to comedy, lectures and musicals. Not quite as grand as the Apollo but at the same time less mainstream.

Plays at the Colleges

Many of the colleges put on theatre in the summer season. Some, like Wadham, have their own theatres while others will put on performances in their gardens and quads, weather permitting. Most colleges advertise on boards outside the college entrances and on posters around town. Failing that, Tourist Information should be able to give details of daily performances as and when they're happening. Students tend to stick to fairly traditional stuff like Shakespeare and Marlow and on a warm summer's evening, can be a sublime experience even if your King Lear is a skinny 18 year old with bumfluff.

CINEMAS

From Art-house cinema to the Hollywood blockbusters, Oxford can cater for all your celluloid needs. Here's how.

ABC
Magdalen Street and George Street (01865) 725305 and 723911

Big commercial releases, blockbusters and none of your poncy sub-titled foreign stuff. This is for people who aren't afraid to stand up and say – *'Actually, I loved Star Wars, it was so well scripted and Ewan McGregor's acting was superb.'*

Can't quite figure out the need to have two similar cinemas a stone's throw from each other but they seem to do well so who am I to grumble? George is like the younger of two brothers who gets all the hand-me-downs after Magdalen has finished with them.

Maison Française
Norham Road
(01865) 274220
maison@sable.ox.ac.uk

If you're a lover of French cinema you might be interested to know that every Monday during term-time at the Phoenix cinema, Maison Française show a range of subtitled contemporary and classic French films ranging from Goddard to Jeunet and Caro. Free to language students, for more details have a look at the Phoenix programme.

The Phoenix
Walton Street (01865) 554909/ 512526
www.picturehouse-cinemas.co.uk

Built in the 1910s this cinema, in the heart of Jericho, has had a colourful history, especially in the 1970s, when, as La Scala, it showed nothing but porn. Today, however, the Phoenix is a popular art-house cinema, running everything from the latest Jim Jarmusch to your favourite cult classic and any sweaty men in raincoats are merely biochemistry students having an evening off.

The cinema also has a café-bar upstairs, where you can hang-out and talk movie-trivia, while on the ground floor you might want to make use of the suggestion box, as they may decide to put on a movie that you've been dying to see for years. The Phoenix even occasionally plays host to directors who, after their new film has been shown, will appear to take questions from the audience.

Immensely popular and by far the best cinema in Oxford it is advisable to book, especially at weekends, when they also show late-night cult flicks.

The Ultimate Picture Palace
Jeune Street (01865) 254288

This place used to show old classic B-movies and cult films but nowadays seems to just show stuff that was out a few months ago but you forgot to see. Generally showing two different films a night the place is a bit run-down and seedy but that's all part of its charm. Once the Penultimate Picture Palace, it used to have these giant Al Johnson hands hanging above it but one day two of the fingers fell off leaving Al giving the two-finger salute to the Cowley Road and so the hands were discretely removed.

Hi there. Im a young Kim Basinger and I would like to tell you about the fun you can have at the PHOENIX PICTURE HOUSE in Oxford. Because they show the best in world and indie cinema you are virtually guaranteed to see either a womans front bottom or a mans dingler dangler on the big screen.
cafe | bar
late night flicks
fab membership scheme
BOOKING LINE (01865) 512526
24 HR INFO (01865) 554909
57 WALTON ST
www.picturehouse-cinemas.co.uk
PHOENIX Picture House Oxford

PERFORMANCE AND COMEDY CLUBS

Catweasel Club
Every Wednesday @roots.net
27 Park End Street (01865) 722227
entry £1.50/ 2.50

The Catweasel Club is something of a legend amongst its followers and performers in Oxford. Principally it's a platform night for local talent where you can expect everything from singer-songwriters to lute-playing, demon fiddlers, classical guitarists and the obligatory poem about one's trip to Goa. If you fancy trying out your latest poetic masterpiece or singing a sea-shanty, these guys will make you feel very welcome (although I do think charging performers an entrance fee seems a little mean-spirited).

The club is run by the very charming and enthusiastic Matt, and strewn with cushions on the floor and flowers on the stage. The atmosphere can be quite intimate and magical at times but it does get busy after 9.30pm so I'd try and get there for 9pm if you want a seat.

As a warning, this is not to everyone's cup of tea; the audience can only be described as a mixed bag of eco-friendly new-agers and earnest old hippies, and if you're cynically-hearted or the kind of person who hates jugglers, you probably won't like this place either. It's the sort of club where smoking roll-ups is compulsory, and mobile phones are still the work of the devil. But if your prejudices can overcome this, or if you fancy performing, I can guarantee you'll have a wonderful evening and meet some friendly people.

Jongleurs Comedy Club
Hythe Bridge Street (01865) 722437
Thurs £8/3 student concs Fri £11 Sat
£13 open until 2am every night

Popular with the mid-thirties crowd, Jongleurs comedy nights seem marketed for those people who feel too old to go to proper clubs but still want to do something different to a night down the local. Not only that, they're probably the only social group prepared to pay the steep weekend prices.

Each night three comedians perform, with the comedy usually finishing around 11pm at which time the disco kicks in. For the first hour it's 80s and Disco classics, again aimed at the thirty-somethings who will get up and dance if Loveshack or La Bamba are playing but might get frightened if Fatboyslim comes on. After they've all gone home at 12.30am to relieve the baby-sitter it usually reverts to chart anthems and a bit of House.

Being part of a nationwide chain, these comedy nights are very formulaic, which does take away the element of danger that keeps comedy fresh. Nevertheless a good comedian is a good comedian, and if you like a bit of stand-up you're most likely to come here on the grounds that there isn't actually anywhere else to go.

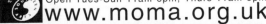

The Oxford Music Scene

The Oxford music scene actually kicked off in 1977 with the release of 'Romeo' by Mr Big but seeing as no one seems to remember it we'll move swiftly on. Let's say it had as much relevance to punk as Steps and leave it at that.

Not surprisingly things were quiet for a few years after that but then, in the mid-80s, came the brief but refreshing C86 scene. Out went the poncy New Romantic bands with their frilly hair and tartan waistcoats and in came tall skinny school-kids sporting floppy haircuts, anoraks, badly tuned Fender Jaguars and singing songs about doing the washing up.

Tallulah Gosh were an Oxford export and were one of the few to survive the scene, transforming first into Heavenly and today, although quiet on the Oxford scene, are still active as Marine Research, having supported Fugazi on their last tour. The band that really came along and really began to put Oxford on the map however were Ride.

Up until the late 80s, this pre-pubescent foursome were little more than Pet Shop Boys wannabes, but after accidentally seeing a My bloody Valentine gig at the Wheatsheaf (believing them to be an all girl Jazz-funk band) it was more than enough to convince the boys that guitar noise and floppy hair was where it was at. Within a year they gave Creation records their first top 75 hit single with the release of the seminal Drive Blind EP.

Inspired also by the likes of Jesus and Mary Chain and Sonic Youth, Ride found themselves at the forefront of what briefly became the Shoegazing or Thames Valley Scene. This was a musical fashion that involved heavy textured guitar sounds, distant vocals, staring at your feet on stage and the necessity to have been born somewhere near Aylesbury.

Ride were also responsible for beginning the craze of featuring a ménagerie of animals and plants on their album covers for no good reason whatsoever. Other champions of the shoe-gazing cause included such charismatic giants of rock as 1000 Yard Stare, Chapterhouse and Slowdive.

It was around this time too that local promoter Mac (with a good ear for the next big thing), was running the Jericho Tavern and regularly featuring early Creation bands such as Primal Scream, as well as the likes of Carter USM and local band On a Friday, all of which were then playing to crowds of little more than 100 in those days.

On a Friday were the early incarnation of Radiohead, who, with Mac's help, attracted the attention of A&R guys, and it wasn't long before On a Friday were signed to a major label. The only problem was their name. The band had chosen this name because they used to rehearse 'on Fridays'. I know, I know, it's hard to imagine this is the same band whose music and lyrics only a few years later would so beautifully describe the dark paranoia and loneliness of the 20th century. After much nagging from the record company, they were eventually given a choice of five names and ordered to pick one by the end of the day.

The choices were:

1) The Muhammed Alis
2) Dearest and Shindig
3) A Horse, a Spoon and a Bucket
4) Radiohead
5) The Happy Chappies

It was a difficult choice but they finally plumbed for Radiohead, the name being derived from a Talking Heads track on The True Stories LP.

After the worldwide success of Creep and a surprise number one in Israel, Radiohead firmly made Oxford the place to watch for the next big thing and it wasn't long before three cheeky young whippersnappers with one enormous eyebrow caught the attention of the music press.

The Jennifers started life in the early 90s as Ride wannabes; I remember seeing them up at Brookes University supporting Slowdive, not thinking they were destined to go far. But before long they'd changed their name, their line-up, and finally stopped putting wah-wah solos in every song much to everyone's relief. The release of their first single, a short but catchy little punky number 'Caught by the Fuzz', took everyone by surprise and they were an overnight success.

The band of course were Supergrass and they secured for Oxford a legacy that nowhere else in England was there such a melting pot of talent.

On the strength of this and with the concerted efforts of local promoters, Radio 1 brought Sound City to Oxford in 1997, and for a short while, even Tony Blair considered packing in politics and re-forming his old Oxford band Ugly Rumour.

Without the emergence of another big name in recent years, Oxford might appear to be losing its touch again but one only has to pop down to the Point or the Bullingdon Arms to see a whole host of bright young things (and not so bright young things) to realise that for a town its size, Oxford still has one of the best music scenes in the country.

POP TRIVIA

Caught by the Fuzz/Strange Ones - Supergrass

You get two for the price of one on Supergrass's debut single. 'Caught by the Fuzz' is the tale of a very young Gaz getting nicked in Oxford for possession of cannabis. The B-side, Strange Ones is a homage to the Cowley Road Care in the Community Centre and all the vagrants that hang out around Methadone park near the Zodiac. I've even been told that their first album 'I should Coco' was inspired by Café Coco at the bottom of Cowley Road but I'm not fully convinced on that one.

Trivia-wise the CD single included a fabulous acoustic version of 'Caught By the Fuzz', but does anyone know why Mickey is holding an egg whisk for the photo that accompanies it?

OX4 - Ride

The last track from their second album 'Going Blank Again', takes its name not from the periodic table but from the band's post-code. It's one of those songs about being away from home too long and missing your girlfriend and your mum's cooking, all with the characteristic swirly guitars and soupy vocals.

Itchycoo Park - The Small Faces

It seems that Steve Marriot and co had been in a few dodgy dealings with some Eastend gangsters and to let things cool down a bit the record company paid for a trip to Oxford to keep them from concrete slipper land. Whilst here, the boys had a jolly nice time and after several spliffs cobbled together the song. Listen out for references to the Bridge of Sighs and Dreamy Spires.

I'm afraid the origins of the title are still a mystery to me, but then they were completely trolleyed when they wrote it.

Radiohead

Although the band did record a song in the early days called 'Million $ question', where Thom expresses his desire to ram-raid his old employers Cult Clothing, no subsequent material has provided titles directly related to Oxford. Listen to the likes of Prove Yourself, Subterranean Homesick Alien and Street Spirit however, and you'll hear Thom eulogising on alienation, pollution, crap housing and god knows what *else to do with the town. Oxford may get a pretty hard time in several Radiohead songs but they all still live here, so it can't be as bad as all that, can it? Remember guys, LA is just a plane flight away…*

Quality But Herſ – Duſtball

Releasing their first album on local label Shifty Disco, Dustball found inspiration from a butcher's shop on the Cowley Road. The shop used to bear the sign 'Quality Butchers' but over time the letter 'c' had fallen down and no-one had bothered to replace it. This was an album title just waiting to happen and these guys had the genius to spot it.

Double Decker – The Bigger The God

About the Oxford park and ride system apparently.
And I think we've gone as far as we can get with this idea.

The Beatleſ and Oxford

Although few people know it, the band did actually come here in the 1960s owing to the labours of Jeffery Archer who then was a hard-working fund-raiser for the University, not the low-life weasel we know him as today. After donating a few items to the college for auction, Archer raised enough money to invite the Fab Four to Brasenose for dinner, and by all accounts everyone had a jolly nice time. It was the only time the Beatles ever visited Oxford in their whole career. There are occasional rumours that they once played a secret gig at the Jericho Tavern in 1968 as a warm up for their aborted 'Paul's Not Dead' tour, but not being one for spurious tales I'm yet to be convinced.

LEGENDS IN THEIR OWN LUNCHTIME

Hairo and the Biros

Formerly the Quiet Men, the Biros once performed the strangest gig I have ever seen in the basement of The Old Fire Station. The gig started well until Hairo, seemingly persecuted by his own equipment, appeared to be getting badly electrocuted by his guitar. Around the same time some bloke in the audience pulled out a bag of diced carrots and for no good reason started throwing them at the band. As the carrots rained down and the electrocutions got worse Hairo did what any self-respecting singer would do and stormed off stage. Years later he moved to London and formed a band called 'Friends of David', a name I'm proud to say I inspired. As you can imagine, I was very keen for them to be famous, as it would have made a great chat-up line, but alas it wasn't to be. Hairo was last seen running a bicycle repair shop in Peckham called 'Can't Get a Grip?'

Arthur Turner's Lovechild

Fronted by the 'terrifying and bald' local legend and promoter Mac, the band have been around since the early 70s and just to annoy everyone are still going strong today. Named after the former caretaker of Oxford United, ATL famously signed to Oxford's Rotator records on the local team's pitch at half-time to the princely sum of £1. I've seen it in writing somewhere that no one is an official citizen of Oxford until they've seen ATL play.

When asked for the philosophy behind ATL, Mac said –

'we make music for other people to listen to and if we like it, it's a bonus.'

The Bigger the God

This weird bunch have been around for many years now, pushing their unique brand of camp, gothic cabaret. Despite brief flirtations with fame on the Big Breakfast and Top of the Pops Two, they never seem to have fitted comfortably into any narrow record label niche, yet remain active for the sheer pleasure of playing together. Their music in recent years has taken more of a turn towards the Jacques Brel school of flamboyance and they seem to be equally loved and hated by those involved in the local scene. It is no small compliment however that editor of Nightshift and NME journalist Dale Kattack recently described their guitarist Ellis as 'the best songwriter in the country'. To see them at their best look out for the next Our Song, where they always pull out the stops.

Swervedriver

Their song 'Son of Mustang Ford' seemed to appear on every Indie compilation in the early 90s and for a short while Servedriver were in fashion. Since then the dreadlocks may have gone but the band are still on the go and recently had a top 70 hit in Papua New Guinea.

ATL show off their 1p cheque

Ronan, Richard, Mac & Dave: the four horsemen of Shifty Disco

LOCAL LABELS AND MAGAZINES

Rotator Records

Set up by promoter and entrepreneur Richard in 1995, Rotator signed up the likes of local hopefuls the Mystics, Sweeney and Arthur Turner's Lovechild and achieved a top forty hit with the Candyskins single 'Monday Morning'. Being pro-active with Shifty Disco, Rotator have remained pretty quiet in the last year or so but with the completion of his new studio on Magdalen Street, Richard may well be on the prowl again for some new talent.

Shifty Disco
(01865)798791 65 George Street
www.shiftydisco.co.uk

Set up in 1997 by Oxford's small but music-obsessive Mormon community, the release of their first single by Dustball and Nought brought instant recognition for the label as both bands found themselves invited to perform a Peel session. From this promising start the label has grown from strength to strength releasing 12 singles and several albums every year. Previous highlights have been from the likes of Mark

Gardner of Ride, Nought and the Unbelievable Truth, and this year also sees the release of the compilation album 'The Sounds of the Suburbs' to tie in with the Channel 4 series.

If that isn't enough to whet your appetite, how could you resist the charm of some of their fruitier offerings such as Spinach, Persil, Murry the Hump and Frigid Vinegar?

Look out for their stuff in the record shops around town, particularly Polar Bear on the Cowley Road. Failing that, get yourself on their mailing list from the above address and hear some of the coolest music this side of the planet.

Nightshift
www.nightshift.oxfordmusic.net

Nightshift www.oxlink.co.uk/nightshift This local free magazine is your bible for what's on, who's worth seeing and all the latest gossip about the local band scene. Heroically keeping the Oxford band scene together, as well as organising events, Nightshift grew from a single piece of A4 written in crayon back in the early 90s, to what it is today a respectable and well-written music magazine (whose founder has even gone on to write for the NME).

Favourite line from Nightshift – 'If white bread could play guitar it would sound like Shed Seven.'

MUSIC EVENTS

Your Song
Twice a year, around 20th August and Christmas

This started about seven years ago at the Jericho Tavern as a bit of fun and has now become a regular twice yearly event where the best of Oxford's local bands try their hands at a few (often outrageous) covers.

Over the years we've seen an early incarnation of Supergrass play Disney songs, Radiohead in a moment of rare humour perform 'Rhinestone Cowboy', 'Money' and 'Hooked on Classics', and the sadly defunct Ultrasound performing the whole of Tommy as a twenty-minute medley complete with full costume and ham acting.

But the band who over the years have contributed the most consistently stunning performances, have to be local legends, The Bigger The God. Everything from Laurel and Hardy's 'Trail of the Lonesome Pine' to Jilted John's 'Gordon is a Moron' have been attempted, not forgetting the time half-way through singing 'My Way', singer David stopped the song, took off his Dr Marten boot and, using it as a telephone, had a chat with the late Frank Sinatra.

As you can see, this is an event not to be missed, keep checking Nightshift for details.

The Punt
Second to last Thursday in May, contact Nightshift for more info

Now in its third year, this is Oxford's answer to the Camden crawl, offering around 20 local bands in different venues around the city giving it their all in one mad afternoon.

VENUES

The Point
The Plain (01865) 262291
Capacity 100ish
Open Thursday-Saturday for gigs

Located above the PubOxford at the bottom of Cowley Road, this moderate sized room with a pretty good PA is probably the best place to discover the next big thing. As well as the local scene you can occasionally catch the odd small touring named bands, cutting edge stuff and the marvelous 'Your Song' which happens here twice a year.

Brookes University
Top of Headington Hill
(01865) 741111 Capacity 1000

Currently Oxford's biggest venue, this is the place to come and see the big boys and has also been a popular spot for the occasional 'secret' warm up gigs from the likes of Blur and Ash. It's a bit of a trek up the hill if you're coming from town but the thought of being so close to those virile young musicians will probably spur you on.

The Jericho
**Above the Fridge Magnet and Firkin
37 Walton Street (01865) 554501**
Once the legendary Jericho Tavern which helped break so many well-known bands, now, with promise of a re-vamp and a decent PA, the Jericho may well be on its way to reviving some of its former glory, and, as a decent 150 capacity venue, help put Jericho back on the local music scene.

Roots.net
**27 Park End Street (01865) 722227
www.roots.net**
Built on the sight of the old jam factory, this multi-purpose world-music venue is open every night of the week. At weekends it puts on an impressive range of music in its venue, the Golden Bough, ranging from folk-

singers to Salsa bands and percussion acts. Attracting not only Oxford's Folk/ Hippy community, it seems popular with anyone who has a passion for world and folk music, and can make a pleasant change from seeing yet another guitar-band at The Zodiac.

As well as organising music workshops at weekends it also has a café and a musical instrument shop, and plans are afoot to open an in-door market and record shop soon.

For the Zodiac and the Bullingdon Arms see club reviews

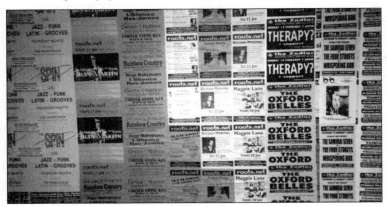

INSTRUMENT SHOPS

Music Box
Cowley Road (01865) 204119

Run by the ex-singer of Go West, this tiny second-hand music shop at the bottom end of Cowley Road is crammed with everything from guitars and amps to second-hand sitars, mandolins and even an original boxed Rolf Harris Stylophone. The guys in here seem up for a haggle so if you share a fag with them and tell them how much you loved 'We close our eyes' they'll probably do you a good discount. Also a good spot for looking for band members, as the door is always littered with ads.

Professional Music Technology
Cowley Road (01865) 725221

The best selection of guitars, amps, drums, effects and computer

technology in Oxford (although the competition is hardly tough).

They seem to specialise in Peavey and Marshall amps and will do a good part-exchange deal for your crappy old original AC 30.

Most likely to say -

'Oh it's great little piece of equipment that is, the guys from Radiohead bought a couple of those last week mate.'

Least likely to say-

'the bloke over the road from Go West used to use that keyboard.'

The Music Room
**At Roots.net 27 Park End Street (01865) 722227 www.roots.net
Mon-Thurs 10am-6pm, Friday 10am-8pm, Sat 10am-6pm, Sun 12pm-4pm**

Impressive collection of acoustic Folk instruments ranging from banjos, fiddles, mandolins and bouzoukis to accordions. Run by Bill and John, expect a good natter about the folk scene and Bill might even share his enthusiasm for real ale and narrow boats if you're not careful. Also stocking tutor books and CDs, the cheapest thing you'll find here are Morris bells for 26p while their most impressive instruments are their range of handmade Heartwood guitars, which Bert Jansch took a fancy to recently. Friendly and well informed, if you're looking for a quality traditional instrument there's nowhere in Oxford better than these guys.

ENGLAND

Squeaky frog used as a toy. The
frog contains a small free reed
which squeaks when it is pressed.

d.d. H. La Rue, 1986.

Oxford in the Books & Movies

Shadowlands
Dir. Richard Attenborough 1993

Set in the 1950s, this is the slow, atmospheric tale of CS Lewis, played by Anthony Hopkins, and the surprising but tragic love-affair he had late in life with an American admirer, Joy Gresham. There are plenty of scenes of Magdalen college and the Cloisters as well as May morning and even Lewis and his writers' group, The Inklings, down the Eagle and Child (except it isn't really). Quite a simple, uncluttered film for Attenborough, with Hopkins sympathetically playing Lewis as a man who learns to suffer and love by liberating himself from the sheltered life he has built.

Oxford Blues
Dir. Robert Boris 1984

Rob Lowe plays a tiresome and obnoxious American who wangles his way to the University where he woos a rich young lady and is properly 'educated' by fellow students in the art of rowing and saying 'okay ya'. Insulting, boring and with surprisingly few shots of Rob Lowe in the nude. Retitled by Time Out as 'A wank in Oxford'.

Wilde
Dir. Brian Gilbert 1997

A rather tepid account of Wilde's ill-fated and illegal relationship with Alfred Lord Douglas. Stephen Fry plays a surprisingly lame Oscar Wilde and even the occasional shots of Jude Law's bottom do little to relieve the monotony of it all. Wilde's old college Magdalen gets a brief look in, and the scenes of Wilde's imprisonment were filmed in Oxford jail shortly after it was vacated by the prisoners.

The Young Sherlock Holmes
Dir. Barry Levinson 1988

Shots of Radcliffe Square and other parts of Oxford come into this tale as a pre-pubescent Holmes and Watson try and discover why an Egyptian loony has been going around killing everyone. Worth seeing just to witness the scene where a malevolent hat-stand comes to life. The scriptwriter must have been on something that day I reckon.

'Hey guys I've got it. The perfect villain. An evil hat-stand!

What? You don't like the idea?

Wait a minute, smoke this...'

Accident
Dir. Jospeh Losey 1967

Dirk Bogarde plays a fellow of Magdalen college obsessed with one of his female students and as the theme of infidelity slowly becomes apparent it moves through the lives of the people around him, gradually pulling them apart. With a tense script from Harold Pinter, the film is pieced together with stilted conversations and pregnant pauses and as the rot sets in the characters try to remain terribly English about it all within their calm University surroundings.

A Chump at Oxford (Laurel and Hardy)
Dir. Alfred Goulding 1939

Having inadvertently foiled a bank robbery, the hapless duo are rewarded with a chance to gain a proper education at Oxford. On their arrival the students take every opportunity to lampoon them, until a blow on the head to Stan reveals him to be an English aristocrat who had been suffering from amnesia. The scene in Oxford maze should be enough to convince you that it was all filmed in the studio, but it's still an endearing comedy on the university, with plenty of classic English stereotypical phrases like 'Well done old bean' and 'he's jolly well asking for a punch on the nose.'

Worth seeking out for fans of slapstick, though if you are a Laurel and Hardy enthusiast, it's not one of their best. Look out for the very young Peter Cushing.

The Madness of King George
Dir. Nicholas Hytner 1994

Nigel Hawthorne plays the king with the unruly stools in this moving and occasionally funny historical drama. Shot close to Oxford, the Bodleian library was also used for the House of Commons scenes.

A Fish Called Wanda
Dir. Charles Crichton 1988

This Cleese-scripted comedy has a few scenes filmed at Morrell's brewery in Oxford (as if you cared).

Heaven's Gate
Dir. Michael Cimino 1980

Mansfield college was bizarrely transformed into an American campus complete with stick-on leaves for this 19th century Western.

True Blue
Dir. Ferdinand Fairfax 1996

Based around the 1987 boat race, this film has lots of shots of the river, the boathouses and other parts of Oxford but lets itself down by being desperately dull.

LITERARY OXFORD

Oxford has always had a rich literary history and I read somewhere that over 500 books have been written based around this city although on closer inspection it was found that half of those were by Colin Dexter. The list of famous authors who studied at the colleges is pretty exhaustive and includes such giants as Oscar Wilde, Evelyn Waugh, Percey Shelley and W.B. Yeats, while in more recent years the University has produced the likes of Martin Amis, Ian McEwan and Will Self.

Many of the last century's decades also seemed to have produced different writers groups such as The Inklings, of which J.R.R Tolkein was a member, and The Movement which included Kingsley Amis and Philip Larkin. To mention all the important Oxford literary figures is a book in itself but the two local based writers perhaps most celebrated in Oxford for their work must be CS Lewis and Lewis Carroll.

Lewis Carroll and Alice in Wonderland

Lewis Carroll was the pen-name of Charles Dodgeson, a mathematics lecturer at Christ Church, who, in the late 19th century enjoyed spending time with Alice Liddell, daughter of the Dean of the college at the time. Legend has it the story came about from a boat trip up the River Godstow where Dodgeson took Alice and her sister one summer. The girls begged Dodgeson for a story

and so he spun an-ever fantastical tale of the adventures Alice might get up to in another world.

It is believed that Dodgeson's relationship with Alice may not have been entirely innocent, and the fact that he kept a darkroom in his lodgings and liked to take photos of

naked children does nothing to help appease these allegations. In fact, Oxford author David Horan went as far as to call him *'an emotionally retarded pervert from whom any sensible parents would today keep their children well away.'*

Fans of the book can find a gift shop opposite Christ Church where you can buy everything from Alice postcards to Alice anti-dandruff shampoo. This shop used to be Alice's favourite sweet shop, which Dodgeson re-named the Old Sheep Shop in Alice Through the Looking Glass.

For a modern-day version of Alice in Wonderland, read Automated Alice by Jeff Noon, where Alice falls into a computer terminal and ends up in an alternative Manchester, it's a wonderful twist on the original.

CS Lewis

The author of the Narnia books and Screwtape letters lived and lectured in Oxford for many years up until his death in 1963. Buried at Headington Quarry Trinity church, Narniaphiles frequently still seek out Lewis's grave and can find etchings of Narnia on the church windows. In no way cashing in on the Narnia legend, the church also has a selection of tea towels and mugs for sale on the Narnia theme.

Over the ring-road in Risinghurst, you'll find Lewis Close. At the end on the right is Lewis's house 'The Kiln', and beyond that is the nature reserve said to have inspired the Narnia chronicles, as well as Tolkein's Middle Earth. Follow the path around the stagnant pond up the hill to the right past the wooden building and you'll get a surprisingly good view of the town. Lewis fans might find it a bit disappointing though, as it really isn't all that magical.

through history. While all the other books about Oxford seem to linger far too long on rather tedious architectural facts and dates about colleges, Horan knows that the secret is in the telling of the tale. Highly recommended.

RECOMMENDED READING

Oxford-David Horan
(from the cities of the imagination series)

Eloquently written and packed with wonderful stories and interesting facts, this book outshines all others on the shelves if you want to learn more about the city. Not strictly a guide, the book instead takes the reader on a slow sprawling journey across the city whilst moving forward

Strange Oxford
(Oxford Golden Dawn Publishing)

Discover the Oxford of pagan wells, giants, ley-lines and witches. This wonderful DIY booklet takes the reader to some relatively unexplored corners of the town as well as places to visit in Oxfordshire, from stone circles to chalk figures on hillsides. Some of Oxford's more mystical figures are celebrated too, including Yeats, the Hellfire Club and one-time demonologist Montague Summers, who, legend has it, was turned into a giraffe by Aleister Crowley, 'though Summers did not appear to notice.'
(Best place to find this is the Inner Bookshop)

Subversive Oxford

UNDERGROUND ORGANISATIONS

Oxford has always been a hot bed of political activity, not just for breeding Tory and Labour puppets at the Universities but also for Green campaigners, Squatters Rights groups and countless others. This is the place Earthfirst! started, an organisation which fuelled countless protests and demonstrations as well as Corporate Watch, a magazine investigating dodgy multinationals, and Land is Ours, a land reclamation group run by Guardian columnist and Newsnight favourite George Omnbiot.

Undercurrents
16b Cherwell Street
Oxford (01865) 203662
www.undercurrents.org

With ten videos, an activist's handbook and several awards under their belt, you have to admire the hard work these guys have done. Undercurrent videos are the result of video activists' work from around the world, filming and documenting news that the media would rather we didn't see.

For an alternative tour of Oxford, Undercurrents 5 is a must with a truly comic scene of Tory transport minister Sir George Young being chased around town by restless natives, which helped win them an award. Oxford's biggest street party can also be seen on Undercurrents 6 when 'Reclaim the Streets' turned Cowley Road into one-hell-of-a big festival. You can also look out for screenings at the Ultimate Picture Palace every couple of months by checking local press, or any of the shops like Uhuru up the Cowley Road. If you want to be involved or have video footage you think would be useful to the group, please send it to the address above or contact Paul. Undercurrents 1-10 can be obtained from the address given.

Subverts
www.oxford-
city.demon.co.uk/counterfeet/

If you ever wondered who is responsible for defacing the billboards around town then you have this bunch to thank. Aiming to put a little more honesty into some of the sugary sloganeering of multinationals and crappy car companies, their graffiti can be seen in the Cowley triangle or anywhere a Macdonalds advert is to be found skulking.

Oxyacetylene
(07970) 343486
www.oxford-city.demon.co.uk/oxyace/

Local bi-weekly leaflet found in all good subversive haunts (as usual try the Cowley Road) providing information on up-and coming demonstrations, talks, and diary events for activists and campaigners.

Squatting

Your best places are still around the Cowley triangle although the council are making it harder. If you walk down Cowley Road look for the house decorated on the side with Re-use, Re-cycle. This was once a successful squat until the council turfed everyone out but not before, dangling from ropes three storeys up, the squatters got their message across.

Channel 6

Hardly subversive but caped crusader Bill Heine does his bit for local people in his programme 'Bill saves the world'. Channel 6 was set up with good intentions but is still struggling to find itself and its audience. Other than that, this is local news for local people who enjoy watching documentaries about local carpet factories amidst the occasional snow flurry.

All Saints Convent Church Embroidery Department
Magdalen Road

Widely known to be a front for Oxford's largest gambling den.

Howard Marks
Oxford's most celebrated subversive:

Once the world's most-wanted man, Howard was for twenty-five years the biggest dope-smuggler in the world. This Balliol graduate took a puff of a joint in the 60s and found his vocation in life. Immortalised in the Super Furry Animals song 'Hanging out with Howard Marks', his more recent exploits include setting up the Cannabis Party (you can guess their policies) and endlessly touring and scrounging joints from the audience.

I once saw Marks performing in Brighton several years ago and during the questions and answers at the end, someone asked -

'Did you ever know Bill Clinton while you were in Oxford?'

Marks replied with a twinkle in his eye -

'Yeah, I met him on several occasions. And I happen to know that he did inhale, and plenty more besides. I should know, I sold him the stuff.'

STRANGE SOCIETIES

Oxford seems to have more than its fair share of neo-hippies, pagans, UFOlogists and occultists, so if Aleister Crowley, Mulder and Scully or Tom Baker are your Gods, this might be a good place to start looking.

The UFO Society & Contact Awareness
Contact M Soper (01865) 726908 or Frank Copeland (01865) 730250 after 7.30pm
Box 23 Wheatley

Set up in 1969 by Lord Something-or-other, Contact Awareness has grown to become one of the main archivists of UFO sightings with over 80,000 now under its belt. It organises public meetings, sky-watches and debates, as well as producing four magazines a year for all you budding X-filers. To join it costs a trifling £9 a year and as organiser Michael Soper told me-

'It might attract the odd weirdo, but you can guarantee that at least they'll be interesting weirdos'.

Oxford Centre for Crop Circle Studies
Jeff Ambler (01865) 872628
www.homepages.enterprise.net-hambler-oxcrop99.html

For the last nine years this organisation have been monitoring crop circles in Oxfordshire and beyond, producing a quarterly bulletin and occasionally meeting at that mecca of Oxford weirdness, the Inner Bookshop. What's exciting is that they organise regular flights across Oxfordshire for

Demonstrators down the Cowley Road

viewing this phenomena, occasionally flying further afield to Wiltshire, where you can expect to see around 30-40 crop formations in one journey. Flights are around £30 per hour with a full plane of 4 people.

address, as can Golden Dawn Publishing company who publish books on occultism and witchcraft. For a fact-sheet send a SAE to the above address.

Oxfordshire Pagan Circle
PO Box 250 Oxford OX1 1AP
Mog (01865) 243671

Describing Paganism as 'an exploration of Earth and its sites,' the pagan circle is a a melting pot for Pagans of all shapes and sizes to meet and share their ideas. The group also organise regular events around the festival days of the solstices, equinoxes, Beltane and Halloween as well as just enjoying a pint and a natter down the pub.
For those into the more serious practice of ritual magic, Oxford's Golden Dawn Occult Society (of which WB Yeats was once a member) can be contacted through the same

Aleister shows off his new hat

Despite features in the Daily Express which make out that all Oxbridge students do is rut like rabbits, the truth is most of them are too busy writing essays to ever contemplate an evening of fellatio with a friend. In fact a recent survey on the sexual antics of students revealed that Oxford was the 'least-sexed University in the country.' As for the townsfolk, spend a Friday night at Downtown Manhattan and you'll pray that they don't know what sex is. OK, I'm only kidding but sex doesn't seem to be an issue that the city wears on its sleeve and for a place its size, the topic is all very much hidden away from the public. The thought of an Ann Summers shop opening seems as likely as the next Olympics being held here. Despite this, there are a couple of more traditional sex-shops on the Cowley Road which we include below for any of you wishing to pepper up your sex life or wanting to fantasise about one.

While reviewing one of the shops I had a sudden flashback of the last time I was in there, it was about eight years ago with my ex-girlfriend and we bought a black rubber dildo for her mate who'd just gone single and needed cheering up. But when we visited her a few weeks later we discovered the only use she'd found for it was a novel way of stirring her tea.

Private Shop
54 Cowley Road (01865) 246958
Open 9.30am-8pm Mon-Sat

The usual collection of dildos, 'naughty magazines' and porn flicks, which even come on DVD now for those who like their porn in surround-sound. Speciality-wise they seem to have plenty of foot-fetishist magazines, including the rather excellent Footsie, and a few back-copies of the wonderfully titled 'Huge Tits'. They also have a small selection of gay men's magazines and a few poor quality fetish clothes. 20% student discounts available on 'Hung like a Horse' back issues and other select titles.

Adult Bookshop
86 Cowley Road (01865) 798287
Open 10am-6pm Mon-Sat

Run by the archetypal 'dirty old man' who just seems to sit behind his counter effing and blinding and ogling over his porn films all day. But if you can deal with walking into this 60s Soho time-warp you'll find a wide range of porn flicks for £40 (no idea what the quality is like) and quite a variety of magazines all about a tenner each. There's a very complete selection of bondage and SM, from the glossy likes of Skin 2, to the more DIY likes of Lesbian Bondage and Spanking weekly. Plus they've got a modest range of gay and TV stuff.

Oxford Gay Scene

Oxford has a small but well-established gay scene, accepted by an open-minded population here and kept fresh by a steady influx of new students. While the Northgate Hall in the town centre is its HQ, the gay community itself is spread thinly around Jericho and East Oxford. The Cowley Road area is a popular place to hang out, try pubs like the Elm Tree, Temple Bar and Baba, while the crowds at the Bully and Zodiac seem relaxed about the rampant snogging sessions I've witnessed on several occasions there. To avoid trouble, loitering around George Street at night is not the best idea, although this advice goes out to anyone who shies away from the company of pissed-up morons.

While cruising seems mainly confined to the established gay bars and clubs, lovers of the great outdoors might find that Angel Meadow (by Magdalen bridge) has a reputation as a good meeting spot. But if at the end of the day you still need something more exotic, remember London is only a bus-ride away, or you could always buy a copy of the Cheeky Guide to Brighton and spend a dirty weekend there instead.

PUBS, CLUB-NIGHTS AND MEETING PLACES

The Northgate Hall
St Michael's Street
£10/£5 membership. Club nights usually £2.50/£2 admission

Oxford's gay and lesbian community centre has been on the go for eight or nine years now and as well as producing a monthly fold out on the

Proud to be Gay

local gay scene, also runs gay and lesbian evenings from Thursday to Saturday.

Friday nights are women-only, offering a monthly Easy Listening slot and the occasional special event such as a ceilidh or comedian, while Thursdays and Saturdays are usually mixed.

Your initial reaction on walking into one of the evenings here will probably be – *'oh my god, I've walked into a village hall.'* And while unfortunately resembling a soiree put on by the local vicar, the nights here are well-loved social events and if you're gay and new to Oxford you'll find a welcoming and friendly crowd.

The Royal Blenheim
13 St Ebbes Street (01865) 248011
Attracting a mixed gay/lesbian crowd this central pub has a good atmosphere and tends to get lively at weekends, especially with the pre-Coven crowd on a Friday. This is pretty much the best town pub for young, openly gay locals and students and even has a notice-board in case you're looking for a gay house-share or just fancy joining the women's rugby and football teams.

The Jolly Farmer
Paradise Street (01865) 793759
Oxford's first gay pub, the Jolly Farmer leans clearly towards an established older gay male crowd, but is very welcoming to new faces. It's also got a beer garden and a reputation for good food at lunchtime.

Loveshack
Fridays at the Coven 2
Oxpens Road (01865) 242770
The Coven is one of those tacky 80s clubs modelled on the cave from the 60s TV series Batman with two floors instead of one. Plus you won't find men in satin capes pouring over ticker-tape in the corner.

Loveshack is an evening of tight t-shirts, kitsch music and flashing lights, with the intimate upstairs part of the club turning into a kind of sing-a-long disco area while downstairs is for banging Techno. Although popular with lesbians, the night is very male dominated, and the ladies toilets seem a popular haunt for camp conversations and other leisure activities.

This is without doubt the best place for cruising in Oxford and for men there's everything on offer here; from the lean mean machines wandering around showing off their muscles, to the older beer-swigging types with shirts hanging over their jeans to hide their pot-bellies.

STUDENTS

The LGB society is a good place to make friends and connections, especially if you're coming out.

They also have a drinks night every Thursday in a different college bar, although whenever it's the turn of Oriel everyone seems to be washing their hair that night.
(See contact numbers)

GAY ACCOMMODATION

Try the following below for gay accommodation but don't be surprised if most of the ads turn out to be along the lines of –

'Lesbian non-smoking cat-lover seeks someone to share allotment.'

This is Oxford after all.

Uhuru 48 Cowley Road
(01865) 248249
Royal Blenheim 13 St Ebbes street
(01865) 248011
Magic Café 110 Magdalen Road
(01865) 794604

Contact Numbers

Gay Oxford
PO Box 144 (01865) 251402
Organises talks, walks and other events, more for the late 20s-60s crowd.

Lesbian, Gay and Bisexual Helpline
(01865) 726893

Wayout Lesbian and Gay Youth Group
(01865) 243389

Oxford Lesbian and Gay Centre
Northgate Hall St Michael's St
(01865) 200249

Lesbian, Gay and Bisexual Handbook for Students
available from OUSU

Queer rights committee and Lesbian, Gay and Bisexual Society
(01865) 270777
queerrights@committies.ousu.ox.ac.uk

Mind, Body, Spirit

With everything from floatation tanks to Buddhist temples, and more acupuncturists per square foot than anywhere else in the UK, if you're looking for spiritual nourishment, Oxford's got the lot.

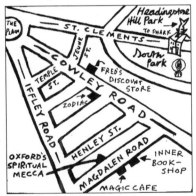

SHOPPING

The Inner Bookshop
111 Magdalen Road (01865) 245301
www.innerbookshop.com

Once tucked away at the back of a butcher's on the Cowley Road, this shop has grown to become one of the best collections of esoteric and occult literature in the UK. From spiritual sciences to gurus, holistic medicines to mythology, the stock is incredibly comprehensive and with a handsome collection of second-hand stuff, much of it is easily affordable. Add to that a meaty selection of CDs, self-help cassettes and postcards and you have New Age heaven.

Like the notice board in the Magic Café next door, theirs is also a good spot to learn more about courses that promise to 'get you in touch with your real self' and 'meet like-minded spiritual souls who share a fondness for Bruce Springsteen.'

I really can't recommend this shop enough, I have bought countless books from here over the years and always consider it a treat whenever I go back. If it just sounds too perfect try getting a smile out of some of the guys who work here.

Neils Yard Remedies
5 Golden Walk Cross Cornmarket Street (01865) 245436

Comprehensive stock of essential oils, herbs, vitamins, homeopathic remedies and self-help books. The staff will give advice on any common illnesses and may be able to recommend practitioners for anything more serious.

ORGANIC/GM FREE AND HEALTH FOOD

Alcock's Butchers
273a Banbury Road Summertown
(01865) 515658

Additive free meat, organic dairy, fruit and veg.

Uhuru
48 Cowley Road (01865) 248249

Wholefood, organic produce, non-dairy produce, gluten-free, yeast free, cruelty free, born free, I'm free (sorry got a bit carried away there) and body products. Their organic apple pies, organic mint chocolate and home-made flap-jacks come recommended and well-sampled.

Gibbons Bakery
16 Hertford Street (01865) 241136

Don't let the name put you off, you won't be finding black hairs in your baps. Mr Gibbons has been working

here for 37 years now, so you could say he's a man that knows his bread. As well as being one of the few places to sell fresh organic bread in Oxford, they also do the very marvellous Cotswold Crunch. The shop is ridiculously tucked away off Magdalen Road but if you're in the area or a sucker for a warm fresh loaf, I wouldn't hesitate to recommend it.

CLINICS AND DROP-IN CENTRES FOR COMPLEMENTARY HEALTH

Eau De Vie Floatation Centre
34 Cowley Road (01865) 200678
Open Tues-Sat 10am-9.30pm, Sun
12pm-7pm £26 For a 1 hour
floatation, £18 student discount
www.eaudevie.co.uk

If you've never been in a floatation tank, it's one of those experiences everyone should try. You climb into what my friend Pete described as a glorified skip, gentle music plays for ten minutes then you're left floating in the dark in Epsom salts, feeling like Major Tom. All senses are cut-off and you will see and feel nothing as you lie there (earplugs and butt-plugs are available for serious floaters). Apparently 90% of brain activity revolves around stopping us falling over under the influence of gravity so floatation is something of a night off down the pub for this stressed organ. Go on, treat your brain to a holiday.

The WellBeing Clinic
6 Kingston Rd
(01865) 311704
Open 9am-5pm Mon-Fri

Continue down Walton Street past the Phoenix cinema and you'll eventually find this place. Probably the most comprehensive collection of complementary medicines in Oxford with everything from Acupuncture to Homeopathy, Alexander technique, massage and more. Some therapists will do cheap rates for low wage earners. Rumoured to be moving soon.

Focus 4 Health
235 Cowley Road (01865) 790235
Open 9am-6pm Mon-Fri
10% discount for students

Another popular clinic for complementary medicines ranging from Osteopathy to Aromatherapy. They've also got rooms you can rent if you fancy giving a slide-show on colonic irrigation.

YOGA, MEDITATION AND BUDDHIST CENTRES

Thrangu House Buddhist Centre
42 Magdalen Road (01865) 241555

These guys have been around in Oxford for 20 years but only moved to this centre a year ago so the building is still under construction. They've got a lovely shrine room for meditation and prayers with under-floor heating so your meditations aren't any more difficult than they have to be. Meditations and pujas are often led by their resident Tibetan Buddhist.

Regular classes include:
Beginners meditation
Tue 7pm-8.15pm
Puja Wednesday
7.30pm-8.30pm and
Sunday 7pm-8.30pm
This is a long prayer where you chant in original Tibetan text. Don't worry though, they give you the English and phonetic translation and a little red kindergarten table to stick your words on. Probably not the best way to get an introduction to this religion though, as I still found myself getting lost and confused.

Oxford Zen Group
The Plain (01865) 240196
Call Rosemary Cottis after 6pm
www.zen-izauk.org Mondays £1

This Soto Zen group, linked to the UK International Zen Association, meet every Monday for group meditations.

Prasangika Buddhist Centre
Friends Meeting House 43 St Giles
Every Thursday 7.30pm-9.30pm £4

Breathing meditation classes and teachings in Buddhism.

Friends of the Western Buddhist Order
18 Bhandari Close (01865) 777297

Run courses in meditation and other stuff.

Pilgrimages
Tel Richard Yeo on
(01235) 534659 for more details.
www.pilgrimage.fsnet.co.uk

Take a six-day pilgrimage through local historic and sacred landscapes

The side effects of tofu can sometimes be quite alarming

from the mysterious stone circles of Avebury to the beauty of the Cotswolds and finishing off not at Oxford ice-rink but the beautiful Pilgrims house in Abingdon. This is a chance to leave all your worries behind and join other like-minded people as you are encouraged to walk mindfully and in the moment. For the Julian Copes amongst you, the pilgrimages often follow a variety of ley-lines taking in neolithic sacred sites and churches. The evenings are spent in top banana B&Bs and peppered with poetry sessions and various talks. Prices are usually around £290 but there is a small discount for students and low-wage earners.

WHERE TO FIND OUT MORE

Green Pages 2000 £3

You'll find copies of this publication in places like the Tourist Information centre and shops up the Cowley Road. It has everything from complementary medicine and counselling to conservation groups, veggie shops and yoga classes.

The Notice Boards at the Inner Bookshop and Magic Café
Magdalen Road

These are always crammed with adverts for healers, therapists, pagan groups, music events and other stuff. Plus, if you're after something yourself, you can stick up your own ad.

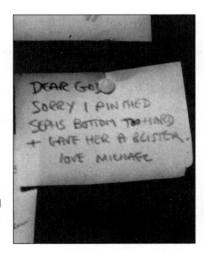

Where to Sleep

16th century cottages with flowery duvets, exotic palatial boudoirs or a rickety sofa bed in someone's garage shed, Oxford has a wide range of accommodation for the most hardened traveller to the comfort seekers with more money than sense.

While there are many hotels and guest houses scattered all over the town, the majority of these lie on Iffley Road and Banbury Road and appear to be run by an army of old women who:

- have been cloned by the city council
- are all called Betty
- will try and sell you their home-made jam and moan about how everyone seemed happier during the war.

It is worth noting that during the summer months it can become very difficult to get weekend rooms here without booking well in advance and if you just show up in June during Henley Regatta or Garsington Opera hoping for the best, you might do well to bring a sleeping bag.

EXPENSIVE

The Old Bank
92-94 High Street, Oxford OX1 4BN
(01865) 799599
info@oldbank-hotel.co.uk
USA Toll free on 0800-544 9993

If not the best hotel in Oxford, then certainly the most urbane. Avoiding all that fake Olde English nonsense that you have to endure in most places here, the Old Bank have instead gone for a modern, stylish layout and every room comes with a large screen TV, full Internet connection and your own CD player with an assortment of very lame music (unless Kenny G is your idea of sonic craftsmanship). The rooms are of course spotless, the staff excellent and your only reasonable objection could be the price.

Occupied by a ghost that lives in the old part of the hotel from the days when it was Barclay's Bank, the staff tell grisly tales of the nocturnal spectre drifting into guests' rooms at the stroke of midnight and trying to sell them house insurance.

The cheapest single occupancy is £135, Doubles start at £155 and there are a few suites ranging between £255-£300, all fees include VAT but breakfast is extra.

The Old Parsonage
1 Banbury Road, Oxford OX2 6NN
(01865) 310210
oldparsoxon@bestloved.com
Toll free from USA 0800 5449993

Located very close to town and with a reputation for being among the finest hotels here, the Old Parsonage is straight out of a Helena Bonham-Carter costume drama with all the rooms lovingly restored to their original 17th century design. The antique furniture and abundance of flowery patterns everywhere won't be to everyone's liking but will probably make American tourists go weak at the knees.

The hotel has a wonderfully colourful history, with famous guests ranging from Michael Caine to Oscar Wilde, who, after returning home late from a heavy Uzo session in Greece, was kicked out of his room at Magdalen College and forced to take up residence here.

Singles £130, Doubles £150-175, Suites £200 inclusive of VAT and full breakfast.

A room at the Crazy Bear

The Randolph
Beaumont Street, Oxford, OX1 2LN (0870) 400 8200 heritagehotels_oxford.randolph@forte.hotels.com

The Randolph is considered by many to be the élite hotel in Oxford and seems to be the favourite destination of the rich and famous. Val Kilmer stayed here for the filming of The Saint, and booked in under the name Simon Templar; the film Shadowlands with Anthony Hopkins was shot here, (although he opted to stay at the backpacker hostel) and Tony Blair used to drink here when he was at the university.

Despite all the fame and fortune the hotel is undoubtedly very good but its reputation far exceeds its quality.

They've even got one of those horrible teddy bears in a graduation outfit sat in the hallway. Eurgh.

Singles £140, doubles £170 and deluxe suites a snip at £400.

Crazy Bear
Bear Lane, Stadhampton, Oxfordshire OX44 7UR (01865) 890714

Located ten minutes drive out of Oxford, The Crazy Bear is a hotel from heaven. All the rooms here are decked out in wild colours and two of the cottage rooms have entirely stainless steel bathrooms. The rooms don't have the normal amenities such as telephones or coffee machines but that's little price to pay compared to the stylish design and beauty of the place. The Monte Christo Suite here has been voted the sixth most romantic hotel room in the world and rumour has it that Richard Gere first fell in love with a hamster here.

If you are arriving at night be careful not to fall over the tree just to the right of the green lights.

Singles start at £60, Doubles at £80. There are five Double rooms, two Cottage Rooms, and they fill up very fast.

If you are planning on a night of romance in the Monte Christo room it's best to book at least six weeks in advance.

MEDIUM PRICED

Burlington House
374 Banbury Road, Oxford, OX2 7PP
(01865) 513513
www.burlington-house.co.uk
stay@burlington-house.co.uk

This wonderful guesthouse is tastefully decorated (not a flowery pattern to be found) and immaculately clean. If travelling alone try and get the single room in the little Japanese garden as it is really beautiful. All rooms come with TV, coffee-making facilities etc but be warned, there is no smoking allowed anywhere within a three miles radius of the hotel and anyone caught having a crafty fag in the toilet will be nailed up as an example to all other guests. It's a fair old walk to town from here but if you're really nice owner Tony will load you up with jars of homemade granola and biscuits for the journey. As far as medium priced accommodation goes this couldn't be better.

Singles £33-48, Doubles £65-70

The Galaxie Hotel
180 Banbury Road, Oxford, OX2 7BT
(01865) 515688

The antithesis of stuffy English hotels, the Galaxie is instead lively, fun, colourful and is an excellent place to stay, especially in summer.

The layout is very enticing with a bright breakfast area, sprawling patio and a back garden, which is home to a family of Coi carp and littered with bonsai trees, which at night attract many of Oxford's pixies community and their dogs.

Singles £50, Doubles from £72

Eurobar
48 George Street,
Oxford, OX1 2AQ
(01865) 725087

Located pretty close to the train station and more or less connected to the bus station, the Eurobar is a good place for the weary traveller to stop and rest for the night. This is a young, friendly place with a café to lounge about in during the day, a cheap and cheerful bar and while the rooms are not overly exciting they're certainly very clean. A good place to stay for younger travellers looking for a little more privacy than a hostel.

Singles £45-55, Doubles £58-69

Pinecastle Guest House
290-292 Iffley Road,
Oxford, OX4 6JU
(01865) 241 497
stay@pinecastle.co.uk

For demonologists and lovers of creepy stories this is the guesthouse for you. Previously owned by Christina Hole, the author of many witchcraft, black magic and folklore-type books, this building has a few dark tales to tell. Even though Mrs Hole died in 1987, there is still a collection of her works on the bookshelf in the bar and the owners can fill you in with stories about her and the darker side of Oxford. The rooms are clean and all come with a TV, phone, hairdryer and cauldron.

Twins £65 or
£55(for one person)

CHEAPER PLACES

Brenal Guest House
307 Iffley Road, Oxford, (01865) 721561

A very agreeable non-smoking B&B close to the city centre offering good meals. The owner gives a great account of one guest, who, having returned late to the hotel found that he had forgotten his keys, so being resourceful decided to procure himself a ladder and climb up onto the roof and in through his window. This would have been a happy ending if it weren't for the screaming German backpackers who didn't appreciate him climbing into bed with them. Favourite guests seem to be parents of students, and least favourite seem to be the 'demanding Yanks'.

Singles £30, Doubles £45

Parklands Hotel
100 Banbury Road, Oxford OX2 6JU
(01865) 554374

While there is no Basil, no Polly, no Manuel, no Sybil, no rats and no German guests, this place still feels inexplicably like Fawlty Towers. Maybe it's just the layout, I really don't know. The rooms are clean, the menu looks good and it's all generally bright and cheery. Most of the 18 rooms have en suite bathrooms, colour TVs, and tea and coffee makers.

Of course you can't see Cowley Beach from here but the manager suggested maybe we *'take a hotel closer to the sea or preferably in it.'*
Singles £38-52, Doubles £68-76

Oxford Backpackers
9a Hythe Bridge Street, Oxford
(01865) 721761
www.hostels.co.uk

As backpacker hostels go, this is pretty standard. There is an excellent pool table, two internet terminals, some video games, and a good collection of books to keep you occupied. Throughout the building colourful paintings adorn the walls, while Reggae music plays through the sound systems, and can even be heard in the bathrooms, helping mask the occasional noises of randy young couples.

Owner Dale is a wealth of information on what to do for your stay in Oxford, although you'll probably spend a few of your nights at the hostel, as having a licence for alcohol means that many, many, many heavy nights of drunken partying take place here. There is even a very helpful job board located in the common room with plenty of listings of local employment etc. Comes recommended.

Dorm rooms only at £11pn, £60pw

Parklands Hotel

YHA Youth Hostel
32 Jack Straw's Lane, Headington
(01865) 762997

Self-catering, single rooms and dorms, a TV room and thankfully no curfew. Commonly associated with the blue anorak brigade, this Youth Hostel is less stereotypical than most but is still a haven for school parties and first time back packers. And you can't even smoke dope here.

To find it, take bus 13 from the bus stop at St Aldates (Every 5-7 min) ask the bus driver to let you off at the end of Jack Straw Lane and point you in the right direction.

£6.85 pn for under 18's and £10 for old fogies

The Courtfield
367 Iffley Road, Oxford
(01865) 242991

The Gabi Roslin of B&Bs. Clean, tidy and nice but in need of a personality.
Singles £34-38, Doubles £44-48, Family rooms £56-63

CAMPING SITES

Oxford Camping and Caravans Club
426 Abingdon Road, Oxford
(01865) 244088

Open all year round, prices range from £3.75-£5.30 per person, per night, depending on the season. 1.5 miles from city centre, this members club is open to any visitor (provided they pay a non-members (£4.30 pitch fee), has 84 pitches that take tents, trailer tents and caravans, and provides on-site showers, toilets and laundry. Although they do take backpackers, two nights is usually the maximum stay and gangs of more than three men might find themselves turned away.

Busy Season

As there is always a chance that all of the above places have no vacancies we have listed numbers below of other places that are recommended by the Oxford Tourist board.

Iffley Road

Ascot Guest House 283 Iffley Road, (01865) 240 259 Vegetarian
Acorn Guest House 260 Iffley Road (01865) 247 998
Bravalla Guest House 242 Iffley Road (01865) 241 326
Bronte Guest House 282 Iffley Road (01865) 244 594
Brown's Guest House 281 Iffley Road (01865) 246 822
Heather House 192 Iffley Road (01865) 249 757
Isis Guest House 45-53 Iffley Road (01865) 248 894 / 242 466
Milka's Guest House 379 Iffley Road (01865) 778 458
The Balkan Lodge Hotel 315 Iffley Rd (01865) 244 524
Palace Hotel 250 Iffley Road (01865) 727 627

Banbury Road

Five Mile View Guest House
528 Banbury Road(01865) 558 747
Holly Bush Guest House
530 Banbury Road (01865) 554 886
Lonsdale Bed and Breakfast
312 Banbury Road (01865) 554 872
Ryans Guest House
164 Banbury Road (01865) 558 876
Adams Guest House
302 Banbury Road (01865) 556 118
Casa Villa Guest House
388 Banbury Road (01865) 512 642
Cotswold House
363 Banbury Road (01865) 310 558

Headington

Mulberry Guest House
265 London Road (01865) 767 114
Mount Pleasant Hotel
76 London Road (01865) 762 749
Pickwicks
5-17 London Road (01865) 750 487
Sandfield House
19 London Road (01865) 762 406

Out of Oxford

Woodstock and Blenheim Palace

8 miles from Oxford (01993) 811091
Park open every day 9am-4.45pm
Palace 10.30am-4.45pm

Named after the bird in the Peanuts cartoon, Woodstock is the kind of English village that American tourists go weak at the knees for, and with Blenheim Palace on its doorstep, is perfect for an afternoon's visit.

For £2 each you can visit the park all day which has a boating lake in the centre, a bridge with thirty rooms and a summerhouse built inside it, and plenty of places to walk to.

The palace and grounds, designed by Capability Brown, are where Winston Churchill was born and are now owned by the Marlboroughs, given to them as a gift from Queen Anne for beating the Dutch back in the 18th century. The front door of Blenheim Palace has the biggest lock in the world, the enormous key of which used to cause no end of grief to Churchill. He would always keep it in his right hand trouser pocket and this is why in photos his trousers always seem to hang to the right in an alarming fashion. If you enjoy nosing

around someone else's house the charge is a hefty £9 for adult, and £5 for children.

In a separate part of the park you can pay another £1.50 to run around a maze as well as marvel at other things like their human sundial and various puzzles.

A good way to enjoy Blenheim is to get together a big group of friends, a huge picnic, some booze, a frizbee and find a good spot to flop around. For the more frugal, you can even get in free through a public right of way situated near The Black Prince pub at the far end of Woodstock.

For anyone interested in such things, Winston Churchill's Grave can be found in the church graveyard in Bladdon, a small village just before Woodstock on the right.

The Uffington White Horse & Dragon Hill

Both visible on the B4507, between Woolstone and Kingstone Lisle, just past Wantage. Parking available.

The White Horse is *'the loveliest of all great British hill-figures'* according to modern-day mystic Julian Cope. This 120 yard-long horse (which arguably looks more like a cat) dates back to 100BC and can be seen clearly from a lay-by. For the full experience you will need to bring with you some Tupperware containing limp salmon sandwiches and a flask of tepid tea to consume whilst viewing this Neolithic marvel.

Nearby, Dragon Hill is a natural cone-shaped hill and the legendary place where St.George killed the dragon. The chalky bald bit on top is said to be where the Dragon's blood fell and no grass has grown there since.

The Sculpture Park, Christmas Common

Always open and great for kids.
To find it take the B480 through Stadhampton to Watlington, through the town centre and then take the little road on the right up the hill to Christmas Common. Turn left at the top of the hill and keep your eyes open for a carpark on your right (it's about ½ hour drive from Oxford and three hours by space-hopper).

Perfect if you want to do something different one Sunday afternoon. The park has over 20 sculptures dotted around its woodland including mirrors in trees, strange towers, things you can climb on and things you can bang.
Henry Moore would have approved. Bring a picnic and a camera.

Shotover Country Park

Just on the outskirts of Oxford up past Headington. To find it go along Old Road and up over the ring road to the top of the hill.

This vast park, a short drive from the city, offers nature walks, mountain bike trails, trees to climb, picnic areas and occasional special events such as the egg-rolling competition at Easter.

Harcourt Arboretum

(01865) 343501
Just down the A4074, a little past Nuneham Courtenay
Open daily except Sundays
10am-5pm May-Oct
10am-4.30pm Nov-Apr

Close to Oxford and ideal for an afternoon jaunt to clear alcoholic cobwebs. Its winding paths through various flora and tree environments are worth visiting any time of year except perhaps February but, let's face it, nothing looks good in February.

Diary of Events

International Women's Festival
End of February to mid-March
(01865) 553755

Always centred around 8th March, (International Women's day), this three-week festival aims to celebrate women's achievements and struggles all over the globe through dance, theatre, music, and poetry in numerous venues around the city. Most events are open to both men and women.

Torpids and Eights
Wednesday to Saturday first week in March and June
(01865) 790268

Inter-collegiate rowing races held on the river Isis to weed out the mice from the men. In summer the turn out is impressive, with especially large crowds turning up on the Saturday to witness the event along the river between Donnington Bridge and The Head of the River pub. Bring a picnic and join the throngs for an afternoon's bumping.

On the last day of Eights it is customary to throw in the cox (the one who sits at the top of the boat and hurls abuse at the crew for not rowing hard enough). The only requirement to cox is to be small with a large voice. But then you know what they say, (cue drum roll)

'Big mouth, small cox.'

Oxford/Cambridge University Boat Race
End of March, beginning of April
(0207) 4657037 for more information

This famous race takes place not in Oxford but along a four and a half mile stretch between Putney and Mortlake in London. Usually taking place late afternoon on the last Saturday in March, this event is regularly watched by up to 250,000 spectators along the banks of the River Thames. Overall, Cambridge is currently in the lead with 76 wins to Oxford's 69 but they also hold the record for sinking the most, at four sinks to Oxford's measly two, although in 1912 both teams somehow managed to sink at the same time.

Poohsticks World Championship
End of March
(01491) 838294
Starts noon at Days Lock Little Wittenham

Grown men and women from all over the world come to throw twigs off a bridge in the hope of winning this coveted title. You can even bring along your favourite Teddy bear and an expert 'teddyatrician' will give advice as to age, value and any necessary surgery. Remember this is for charity so no cheating please, the contestant who brought a stick with a tiny motor hidden inside last year has only recently been released from prison.

Contact Sinadon Rotary Club in Wallingford for more details and how to enter.

Zippos Circus
Usually Tues-Sun, middle of March.
(01865) 726871 for more details

Hosted every year by Papa Lazaru, the acrobatics and other mischief usually take place in the grounds of the Ice rink or South Parks. This may be a cruelty-free non-animal circus but the clowns are kept in appalling conditions, being forced to drive dangerously decrepit automobiles and made to walk around in unsuitable footwear.

Hard-Boiled Egg Race
End of April
Shotover Plain Carpark
(01865) 715830 for more details

This fine 100 year-old tradition takes place every Easter, involving egg-races and a huge picnic. Bring along some cucumber sandwiches and lashings of ginger beer and of course your own lovingly painted hard-boiled egg. There

Another cox gets a surprise bath

are prizes for the best-painted egg followed by the Demolition Derby. The egg that rolls the fastest and furthest down the hill is the winner but watch out for monsters (in the guise of cardboard boxes with mouths) who will eat your egg given half the chance. One year some joker put an explosive in his monster which blew up the first egg that went in.

Gaz from Supergrass used to come to this every year and loved it so much he wrote the song 'Shotover' about it on their third album.

Be in the car-park by 11am with your hard-boiled egg and get ready for what must be the event of the year.

May Morning
May 1st

One of the most important and exciting days in Oxford's calendar. This tradition, to most ignoramuses, simply means that the pubs magically open at 6am, but May morning is in fact an age-old Spring celebration with its roots firmly embedded in the Pagan tradition.

Set your alarm for 5am, drag yourself out of bed and make your way to Magdalen Bridge to witness the college choristers sing carols and madrigals from the top of Magdalen tower. The whole of the High Street is usually mobbed for this and it is quite a spectacle. For centuries students have also followed an age-old tradition by jumping off the bridge into the river but last year the police stopped it on the grounds that it was 'silly' and 'someone might

get hurt' which is of course the whole point.

The choir usually finishes with 'Walking in the Air' and then the bells are rung to greet in the new Spring and around the town you'll see Morris dancers prancing gaily. Some of the more serious Pagan worshippers come out wearing these giant phalluses, as Spring was traditionally a time for celebrating fertility but if you've ever seen The Wickerman' you'll do best to keep well out of their way. Once you've experienced all this, you may by now want to tuck yourself up

in a warm, busy pub and experience the peculiar feeling of getting drunk first thing in the morning. Chances are, by mid-morning you'll want to go back to bed, but your friends will egg you on to have another couple of pints ensuring that the rest of the day will be just a haze, but don't worry, the whole town is usually one huge hangover by mid-afternoon.

A month of Fun in the Parks
May bank-holiday Monday South Parks
(01865) 335488 for more details

Huge crowds regularly turn up for this family event held in South Park just off St Clement's. Expect local bands, a radio roadshow, clowns, fire-eaters, jugglers, bouncy castles and a fun fair.

Balloon Fiesta
Mid-May South Parks

Continuing the Fun in the Parks festival, this weekend event involves parachute drops, dog display teams and majorettes, but don't worry there's some good stuff as well. On Saturday evening a load of hot air balloons are launched high up into the night sky for an event known as 'Nightglow' where the balloons line up and burn torches in time to a Jazz soundtrack from Sun Ra. This is followed by a well-deserved fireworks display.

Lord Mayor's Parade
Bank holiday Monday end of May

Oxford's answer to the Mardi Gras. Starting at St Giles and finishing at South Parks, this procession of floats features everyone from the Bill Heine fan club float to all the local insurance companies who, every year, dress up as black and white minstrels. Look out for the Lord Mayor's float where she sticks on a hula skirt and joins in with the dancing and the fun of it all.

Eights Week
Early May (see earlier listings)

Summer Theatre at Magdalen School
June-September
contact (01865) 250636 for details
Tickets, prices and times available from
Oxford Playhouse
(Prices usually range from £6-£15)

Located just past Magdalen bridge between St Hildas and Christ Church meadow, the plays takes place on a beautiful spot on an island in the river Cherwell. Outdoor theatre doesn't come more magical than this, and the company utilise their surroundings whichever way they can. Previous years have seen actors absailing from trees, arriving in boats, performing from tree houses and occasionally falling in the river.

The company perform two plays each summer, usually six times a week. Until recently they've always done Shakespeare but this year they'll be branching out with what promises to be a truly stunning version of 'Alice Through the Looking Glass', with the audience following Alice on her adventures around different locations on the island.
Evening performances vary in time, usually starting between 7pm-8pm but it's best to contact the box office for details. This is an event not to be missed.

Encaenia
Falling on the Wednesday of the ninth
week of Trinity term in June

Witness the annual spectacle of all the college officials parading through town in their Sunday best to the Sheldonian theatre where they bestow honoury degrees to the famous and wealthy.

St Giles Fair

Held the first Monday and Tuesday in September after the first Sunday unless the Sunday is the first. (Don't blame me, I don't make up these rules)

For hundreds of years now St Giles has welcomed this two day fair which brings wonderful chaos to the town centre. It is certainly more for the townsfolk than students as the students are still officially on holiday at this time (although a few do sneak back early to do some girly swatting).

Expect everything from the old carousel-style fairground rides to the modern ones that scare the willies out of me. Plus there are festival stalls with everything from candy-floss to fortune tellers. Look out for the tattooed lady, she was once a promising undergraduate from St John's but just couldn't resist the lure of the bright lights and men with lamb-chops and greasy hair.

Lord Mayors Christmas Carols

Mid-December
Held in the town hall. (01865) 252838 for more details

Christmas is not Christmas without a hearty rendition of God Rest Ye Merry gentlemen and Rudolph the Red Nosed Reindeer, both of which ought to be on the menu this year. This has to be the perfect way to get yourself into the Christmas spirit, without raiding the drinks cabinet.

Useful Information

Tourist Information Centre
Old School Pub Gloucester Green
(01865) 726871 Open Mon-Sat
9.30am-5pm, Sun10am-3.30pm

Your one-stop destination for booking
hotels, tours, bus trips and finding out
what's on, in and around the city. Sure,
much of the information here covers
the more mainstream aspects of the
city's entertainment and you probably
won't find out who's playing down the
Zodiac tonight but then you might
never have discovered that Elkie
Brooks was in town if you hadn't
popped in.

HOSPITALS

John Radcliffe (Casualty)
Headley Way, Headington
(01865) 741166

Radcliffe Infirmary
Woodstock Road, (01865) 311188
(Ear, Nose and Throat)

Nuffield Orthopaedic
Windmill Road, Headington,
(01865) 741155

Churchill
Old Road, Headington
(01865) 741841

The Acland
25 Banbury Road, Oxford,
(01865) 52081

HEALTH CENTRES

Blackbird Leys Health Ctr
Blackbird Leys Rd, (01865) 246388
Botley Health Unit, West Way House,
Elms Parade

East Oxford Health Centre
Manzil Way
(01865) 242109

North Oxford Medical Ctr
96 Woodstock Road (01865) 311005

Quarry Surgery
248 London Road, Headington
(01865) 761047

South Oxford Health Centre
Lake St (01865) 244428

St Bartholomew's Medical Centre
Manzil Way (01865) 242334

Temple Cowley Health Centre
Temple Road, Cowley
(01865) 7770294

West Oxford Health Centre
Binsey Lane (01865) 246495

LATE-NIGHT CHEMISTS

Boots
6 Cornmarket (01865) 247461
Weekdays until 6pm, and 7pm on
Thursdays

Lloyds
1 Woodstock Road Mon-Fri until 8pm
Sun 10am-5pm

10 O'Clock Pharmacy
59 Woodstock Road
Every day until 10pm

EMERGENCY SERVICES

Police
St Aldates (01865) 26600

Fire
(01865) 242223

ADVICE LINES

Drug & Alcohol Problems
(01865) 226243

LIFE Pregnancy Care Service
(01865) 202435

OXAIDS
(01865) 243389 advice and support on
HIV infection and AIDS

Oxford Friend
(01865) 726893 support/information
for gay and bisexuals.
7-9pm Tues, Weds and Fri only

Oxford Sexual Abuse & Rape Crisis Centre
(01865) 726295

Oxfordshire Counselling Service
(01865) 308999

Samaritans
(01865) 722122

Relate
(01865) 242960

Student Nightline
(01865) 553456 confidential listening
service for students by students, 8pm-
8am (During term)

INTERNET @CCESS

Internet Exchange
12 George Street (01865) 241601
Open 7am to 11pm
www.internet-exchange.co.uk
Access from 3p per minute

Located upstairs from Costa Café, the Internet Exchange provides lots of computers, and row after row of travelers checking hotmail for letters from Mom. Every paper holder, Mouse mat and screensaver seems to be a corporate advert, which is a bit irritating. The layout is comfortable, staff friendly, and it is a treat to be able to get a decent cup of coffee and good food from the café, as opposed to the usual Internet café motor-oil. Downstairs from here is an area laden with comfy couches and large windows, and is ideal for wasting the day people-watching.

Mices.com

118 High Street (01865) 726364
Open 10am until 10pm
www.mices.com
£5 per hour

Recently opened on the High Street, mices.com offers the fastest public access Internet in town by far. If you are looking for a quieter place to get some emailing or surfing done, and can do it without Bob Marley, then I recommend you do your digital traveling here. Download speeds are approx 80k per second (real times) not the usual advertised lies. It may not be the coolest net access, but when it comes to the actual quality of the service, this is the best in town. There are no food or drink facilities here but most users here have mastered the art of chewing the cud.

Mr Pickwicks

13 The Gallery, Gloucester Green
(01865) 793149
£ 4 per hour

Located at the bus station, this is essentially a newsagent with a few coin-operated Internet machines.

Oxford County Council Library

Westgate
(01865) 815509

Open 9.15am-7pm Mon-Sat except for Wed until 1.30pm and Fri-Sat until 5pm
£6 per hour

Mailboxes etc

266 Banbury Road, Summertown
(1865) 514655
Open 8.30am-6pm

One terminal, grossly overpriced at £12 per hour.

For any other wonderful Oxford info that you may need. go to:
www.dailyinfo.co.uk

'Oxford is full of over-qualified milkmen and postmen.'
Bill Heine

'...just a lot of men in duffel coats wandering up and down the High Street.'
Richard Ingrams

'Oxford is the capital of romance.'
Oscar Wilde

'I smoked as much marijuana as I could get my hands on, read Kerouac, listened to Bob Dylan and attended French movies I didn't understand.'
Howard Marks

'Cambridge is much better'
my neighbour Sam Livingstone

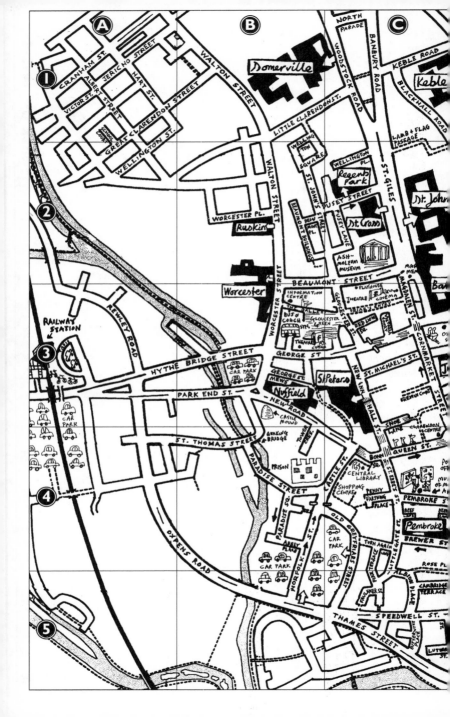

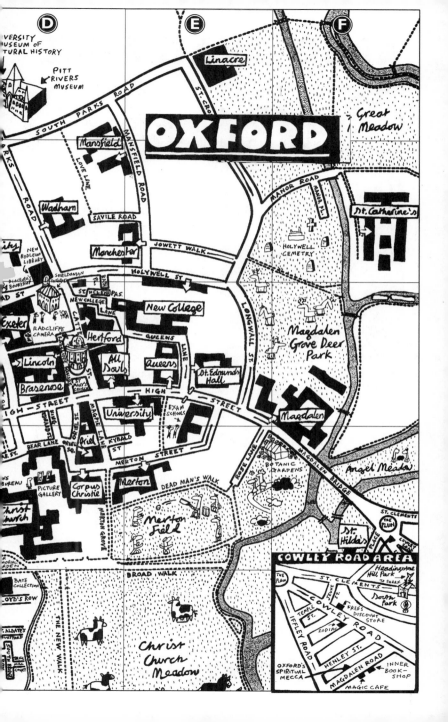

ALSO AVAILABLE

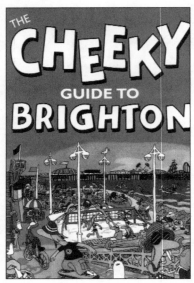

ISBN: 0 9536110 0 0 • £4.99

The Cheeky Guide To Brighton will take you on a factual but comic journey to the many corners of this celebrated town, taking in it's famous nightlife and gay scene, as well as lesser known features such as llama trekking over the Downs and where to contact the dead.

Expect a wealth of funny stories and bizarre characters, as the book dishes out essential information on where to do the best shopping, where to eat the best fish and chips and where to spot your favourite celebrity. Even if you have no intention whatsoever of visiting Brighton, this book is still a must.

Don't walk too quickly round this town because you never know when an adventure might happen. I love Brighton. If you read this book you'll understand why. - Director/ comedian Ken Campbell

'The Cheeky Guide captures the spirit of Brighton perfectly.' Skint Records

visit our website
www.cheekyguides.com